MIPS Assembly Language Programming

MIPS Assembly Language Programming

Robert Britton

Computer Science Department
California State University, Chico
Chico, California

PEARSON

Prentice
Hall

Upper Saddle River, New Jersey 07458

Library of Congress Cataloging-in-Publication Data

Britton, Robert (Robert L.)
  MIPS assembly language programming/Robert Britton.
    p. cm.
  ISBN 0-13-142044-5
  1. MIPS (Computer architecture) I. Title.

  QA76.9.A73B79 2004
  005.265—dc21

                              2003048273

Vice President and Editorial Director, ECS: *Marcia Horton*
Executive Editor: *Petra Recter*
Vice President and Director of Production and Manufacturing, ESM: *David W. Riccardi*
Executive Managing Editor: *Vince O'Brien*
Managing Editor: *Camille Trentacoste*
Production Editor: *John Keegan*
Manufacturing Manager: *Trudy Pisciotti*
Manufacturing Buyer: *Lisa McDowell*
Director of Creative Services: *Paul Belfanti*
Creative Director: *Carole Anson*
Art Editor: *Jayne Conte*
Cover Designer: *Bruce Kenselaar*
Executive Marketing Manager: *Pamela Shaffer*
Marketing Assistant: *Barrie Reinhold*

© 2004 Pearson Education, Inc.
Pearson Education, Inc.
Upper Saddle River, New Jersey 07458

Printed in the United States of America

ISBN 0-13-142044-5

Pearson Education Ltd., *London*
Pearson Education Australia Pty. Limited, *Sydney*
Pearson Education Singapore Pte. Ltd.
Pearson Education North Asia Ltd. *Hong Kong*
Pearson Education Canada Inc., *Toronto*
Pearson Educación de Mexico, S.A. de C.V.
Pearson Education—Japan, Inc., *Tokyo*
Pearson Education—Malaysia Pte. Ltd.
Pearson Education Inc., *Upper Saddle River, New Jersey*

To my daughters, Susan, Nancy, Ann, and Becky;
and to my wife, Jan.

Contents

Related Web Sites

http://www.mips.com/
http://www.ecst.csuchico.edu/~britton
http://www.cs.wisc.edu/~larus/spim.html
http://www.downcastsystems.com/mipster.asp
http://www.cs.wisc.edu/~larus/SPIM/cod-appa.pdf
http://courses.cs.vt.edu/csonline/NumberSystems/Lessons/
http://www.d6.com/users/checker/pdfs/gdmfp.pdf

Preface

This text is targeted for use in an introductory lower-division assembly language programming or computer organization course. After students are introduced to the MIPS architecture using this textbook, they will be well prepared to go on to more advanced courses in computer organization where any modern reduced instruction set computer (RISC) is analyzed. This text provides a technique that will make MIPS assembly language programming a relatively easy task as compared to writing complex Intel™ x86 assembly language code. The skills learned, as a MIPS assembly language programmer, will facilitate learning other more complex assembly languages if the need ever arises. Students using this text will acquire an understanding of how the functional components of modern computers are put together, and how a computer works at the machine language level. It is assumed that students using this text already have some experience in developing algorithms, and running programs in a high-level language.

Chapter 1 provides an introduction to the basic MIPS architecture, which is a modern RISC. Chapter 2 shows how to develop code targeted to run on a MIPS processor using an intermediate pseudocode notation similar to the high-level language C. Once an algorithm is specified in this pseudocode notation it is a relatively simple task to translate it to MIPS assembly language. Chapter 3 is an introduction to the binary number system. This chapter provides simple procedures for converting values from one number system to another. The rules for performing binary arithmetic are explained. Students will learn how to detect when overflow occurs. Chapter 4 explains the features of the PCSpim simulator for the MIPS architecture, which is available for free.

Within the remaining chapters, a wealth of programming exercises are provided that every student needs to become an accomplished assembly language programmer. Instructors are provided with a set of PowerPoint slides. After students have had an opportunity to develop their pseudocode and the corresponding MIPS assembly language code, they can be shown example solutions to each of the exercises via the PowerPoint slides. In Chapter 5, students are presented with the classical input/output (I/O) algorithms that involve converting numbers between their integer binary representation and their ASCII decimal and hexadecimal representation. The utility of logical operators and shift operators are stressed.

In Chapter 6, a specific argument-passing protocol is defined. Most significant programming projects are a teamwork effort. Emphasis is placed on the important fact that everyone involved in a teamwork project must adopt the same convention for parameter passing when calling functions. In the case of nested function calls, a specific convention is defined for saving and restoring values in the temporary registers.

In Chapter 7, the necessity for reentrant code is explained, as well as the rules one must follow to write such functions. In Chapter 8, students are introduced to memory-mapped I/O. The MIPS simulator provides a memory-mapped I/O feature so that students can gain experience in writing drivers that interface with physical devices. With this PCSpim feature, students can gain experience in writing code to communicate character by character with physical I/O devices. The code that communicates with a physical device at this level is often referred to as a driver. This is a significant advantage of using a simulator to learn assembly language programming. Students learning to write native assembly language typically never have an opportunity to write code that interfaces directly with the I/O devices. These students have to be satisfied with making calls to Basic Input Output System (BIOS) procedures that handle the details of communicating with the I/O devices. Typically these students never experience the real-world challenges that arise as a result of the communication and device time delays.

Chapter 9 introduces exceptions and exception processing. PCSpim responds to interrupts generated by the memory-mapped keyboard and display terminal. Given this feature, students have an opportunity to experience writing code to respond to interrupts. Once again this points out the advantage of using a simulator when learning to write assembly language code. Students learning to write assembly language code for their desktop computer typically never have an opportunity to write and run interrupt handlers that enable and disable the interrupt system. Typically these students never experience the real-world challenges that arise in writing the code that resides at the very heart of the operating system.

In Chapter 10 a pipelined implementation of the MIPS architecture is presented, and the special programming considerations dealing with delayed loads and delayed branches are discussed. PCSpim provides an option to run the simulator as if the code were executing on a pipelined implementation of the MIPS architecture. Using this option, students gain experience in writing assembly language code that will run on a pipelined implementation. Chapter 11 provides a description of the floating-point features of the MIPS architecture, as well an introduction to the IEEE 754 floating-point standard.

I would like to acknowledge Bary Pollack, James Gips, Doug Milhous, and Dwite Brown who adopted the earlier draft versions of this textbook. I wish to express my special appreciation to Bary Pollack and Tom Fountain for their thorough review of my initial submission to Prentice Hall, and their many constructive recommendations for improvements. The feedback from Seyed H. Hosseini, and Wagdy H. Mahmoud was also quite helpful. I also wish to thank Petra Recter, senior computer science editor, and John Keegan, production editor, both at Prentice Hall, who so effectively managed this project. I am especially grateful to my wife, Jan, for her support and encouragement. She is my true helpmate and soul mate.

Robert Britton
April 2003

MIPS Assembly Language Programming

CHAPTER 1

The MIPS Architecture

If at first you don't succeed,
Skydiving is definitely not for you.

1.1 INTRODUCTION

This textbook provides a technique that will make MIPS (microprocessor without interlocking pipeline stages) assembly language programming a relatively easy task as compared to writing Intel™ x86 assembly language code. We assume that you have experience in developing algorithms, and running programs in some high-level language such as C, C++, or Java.

One of the benefits of understanding and writing assembly language code is that you will have new insights into how to write more efficient, high-level language code, even if you never write another line of assembly language code again after this course. In learning assembly language, you will become familiar with the task that compilers perform. You will also learn how computers are organized down to the basic functional component level. You may even open new opportunities for yourself in the exploding field of **embedded processors**.

Going to the web site www.mips.com/, you will find that the MIPS processor is used in these systems: Sony PlayStation, Cisco Routers, Laser Printers built by HP and Fuji, PDA's, Set-Top Boxes, Sony AIBO™ Entertainment Robot, and the Minolta Digital Camera.

The first thing everyone must do before they begin to write MIPS assembly language code is to become familiar with the MIPS architecture. The **architecture** of any computer is defined by the registers that are available (visible) to the assembly language programmer, the instruction set, the memory-addressing modes, and the data types.

1.2   THE DATAPATH DIAGRAM

It is very useful to have a picture of a **datapath diagram** that depicts the essential components and features of the MIPS architecture. Please note that there are many different ways that any computer architecture can be implemented in hardware. An initial picture of a MIPS datapath diagram will be the straightforward, simple diagram shown in Figure 1.1. This is not a completely accurate diagram for the MIPS architecture; it is just a useful starting point.

Computers work by fetching machine language instructions from memory, and executing the instructions. In the case of the MIPS architecture all instructions are 32 bits in length. The acronym "bit" is an abbreviation of "binary digit." The instructions are stored in memory locations sequentially one after another. The **machine language** instructions and the values that are operated upon (**operands**) are encoded in binary. Chapter 3 introduces the binary number system. As we progress through the first two chapters of this textbook, we will be expressing values as decimal values, but keep in mind that in an actual MIPS processor these values are encoded in binary.

1.3   BASIC FUNCTIONAL COMPONENTS

The basic functional components of the MIPS architecture shown in Figure 1.1 are as follows:

- control unit
- register file

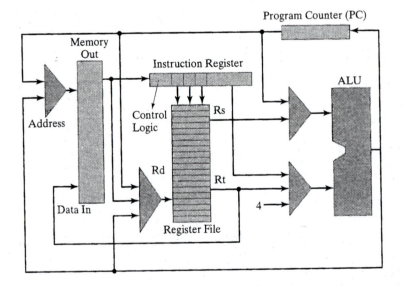

FIGURE 1.1

Mips simplified datapath diagram.

- arithmetic and logic unit (ALU)
- program counter (PC)
- memory
- instruction register (IR)

Interconnecting all of these functional components, except the control unit, are buses. A **bus** is nothing more than a set of electrical conducting paths over which different sets of binary values are transmitted. Most of the buses in the MIPS architecture are 32 bits wide—in other words, 32 separate, tiny wires running from a source to a destination. In this datapath diagram, we have the situation where we need to route information from more than one source to a destination, such as the ALU. One way to accomplish this at the hardware level is to use a **multiplexer**. Multiplexers are sometimes called **data selectors**. In Figure 1.1, data selectors are represented by the triangle-shaped symbols. Every data selector with two input buses must have a single control wire connected to it. The **control unit** sends a control signal of zero or one to select which input bus should be routed to the output. In Figure 1.1, control signal wires are not shown, because it would make the diagram overly complex. When the control signal to a data selector is zero, the 32-bit value connected to input port zero will appear on the output of the data selector. When the control signal is one, the 32-bit value connected to input port one will appear on the output of the data selector. You will notice in Figure 1.1 that there are two data selectors with three buses connected to their inputs. These data selectors will have two input control wires. With a 2-bit control signal, it is possible to select between four different input ports.

1.4   THE CONTROL UNIT

To fetch and execute instructions, control signals must be generated in a specific sequence to accomplish the task. As you have already learned, data selectors must have control signals as inputs. Each register has an input control line, which when activated will cause a new value to be loaded into the register. The ALU needs control signals to specify what operation it should perform—for example, add or subtract. The memory needs control signals to specify when a read or write operation is to be performed. The register file needs a control signal to specify when a value should be written into the register file. All of these control signals come from the control unit. When you take a course in digital-logic design you will learn how to design such a control unit. Suffice it to say that such a control unit can be implemented in hardware to produce a sequence of signals to control the fetching of instructions from memory, and the execution of these instructions.

1.5   THE MIPS REGISTER FILE

Anyone who has ever used an electronic handheld calculator has experienced the fact that there is some electronic component inside the calculator that holds the result of the latest computation. This electronic storage component is called a **register**. Most of the registers in the MIPS architecture have a capacity to hold a 32-bit binary number.

TABLE 1.1   The Register File

Register	Number	Usage
zero	0	Constant 0
at	1	Reserved for the assembler
v0	2	Used for return values from function calls
v1	3	
a0	4	Used to pass arguments to functions
a1	5	
a2	6	
a3	7	
t0	8	Temporary (Caller-saved, need not be saved by called functions)
t1	9	
t2	10	
t3	11	
t4	12	
t5	13	
t6	14	
t7	15	
s0	16	Saved temporary (Callee-saved, called function must save and restore)
s1	17	
s2	18	
s3	19	
s4	20	
s5	21	
s6	22	
s7	23	
t8	24	Temporary (Caller-saved, need not be saved by called function)
t9	25	
k0	26	Reserved for OS kernel
k1	27	
gp	28	Pointer to global area
sp	29	Stack pointer
fp	30	Frame pointer
ra	31	Return address for function calls

The MIPS architecture has a **register file** containing 32 registers. (See Table 1.1.) Each register has a capacity to hold a 32-bit value. The range of signed decimal values that can be represented with 32 bits is $-2{,}147{,}483{,}648$ (-2^{31}) to $+2{,}147{,}483{,}647$ $(2^{31} - 1)$. The process of converting numbers between binary and decimal representation is explained in Chapter 3. When writing at the assembly language level almost every instruction requires that the programmer specify which register file locations will be accessed to obtain operands, and the location in the register file where the result will be stored. A **convention** has been adopted that specifies which registers are appropriate to use in specific circumstances. The registers have been given names that help remind us about this convention. All register names begin with the dollar-sign symbol in MIPS assembly language code. It is recommended that every time you see the dollar-sign symbol you say "register." *Register 0* is special; it is the source of the constant value zero. Nothing can be stored in Register 0. Register number 1 has the name $at, which stands for assembler temporary. This register is used by the assembler to implement **macro instructions** and should not be used by the assembly language programmer. The macro instructions are listed in Appendix D. Registers $k0 and $k1 are used by the kernel of the operating system and should not be used in a user program.

According to the convention, registers 2 and 3 (with the names $v0 and $v1) are used to **return values** from functions. Registers 4, 5, 6, and 7 with the names $a0, $a1, $a2 and $a3 are used to **pass arguments** to functions. The 10 registers named $t0 through $t9 are used to hold **temporary values**. Programmers writing functions typically use these registers. The 8 registers with names $s0 through $s7 are used by programmers when writing a main program to hold values that need to be saved (not modified) while functions are being called. The **stack pointer** register, $sp, is initialized by the operating system to point to a segment of memory called the stack. The **return-address** register, $ra, is loaded with a return address every time the machine executes an instruction to call a function. The register named $fp is the frame pointer. Programmers writing functions use this register to establish a constant reference offset to local variables and function parameters.

1.6 THE ARITHMETIC AND LOGIC UNIT (ALU)

The **arithmetic and logic unit (ALU)**, as its name implies, is a digital logic circuit designed to perform binary integer arithmetic operations, as well as binary logical operations such as "AND", "OR", "NOR", and "Exclusive OR". Which operation the ALU performs depends upon the operation code in the instruction that has been fetched from memory.

1.7 THE PROGRAM COUNTER (PC)

The **program counter** (PC) is a register that is initialized by the operating system to the address of the first instruction of the program in memory. Notice in Figure 1.1 that the address in the program counter is routed to the address input of the memory via a bus. After an instruction has been fetched from memory and loaded into the IR, the PC is incremented so that the CPU will have the address of the next sequential instruction for the next instruction fetch. The name program counter is misleading. A better name would be program pointer, but unfortunately the name has caught on, and there is no way to change this tradition.

1.8 MEMORY

Memory can be thought of as a large array of locations where binary information is stored and from which binary information can be fetched, one "word" at a time. In the case of the MIPS architecture, the term **word** refers to a 32-bit quantity. Each location in memory has a 32-bit address. In the MIPS architecture, **memory addresses** range from 0 to 4,294,967,295 ($2^{32} - 1$). The MIPS architecture uses the term **half-word** to refer to a 16-bit value, and the term **byte** to refer to an 8-bit value. The MIPS architecture specifies that a word contains 4 bytes, and that the smallest addressable unit of information that can be referenced in memory is a byte. The address of the first byte in a word is also the address of the 32-bit word. All **instructions** in the MIPS architecture are 32 bits in length. Therefore, the program counter is incremented by four after each instruction is fetched, so that the program counter will be pointing to the next instruction in sequence.

1.9   THE INSTRUCTION REGISTER (IR)

The **instruction register** (IR) is a 32-bit register that holds a copy of the most recently fetched instruction. In the MIPS architecture, three different **instruction formats** are defined: register format, immediate format, and jump format. The following descriptions apply for the majority of the MIPS instructions. The specific details for each instruction are presented in Appendix C.

   Register format instructions have a 6-bit op-code field filled with zeros. In these instructions, the last 6 bits of the word contain a code to specify what instruction should be executed by the computer. Register format instructions contain three 5-bit fields that specify the register file locations (Rs and Rt) from which the source operand values are fetched and the register file location (Rd) where the result of the instruction operation is stored (destination):

Op-Code	Rs	Rt	Rd		Function Code
000000	sssss	ttttt	ddddd	00000	ffffff

File locat?   *Stores results of instruct?*   *specify instructions to be executed*

The **immediate format** instructions have a 6-bit op-code field where the operation code is stored to specify what operation should be performed by the MIPS processor. The last 16 bits of the instruction word contains a binary value (a constant) that is used as one of the source operands. These instructions contain a 5-bit field that specifies a register file location (Rs) from which a source operand value is fetched and the register file location (Rt) where the result of the instruction operation will be stored. Instructions of this format perform arithmetic or logical operations between a **variable** in the register file and a **constant** value stored within the instruction. Branch instructions, as well as load and store instructions, are encoded in this format:

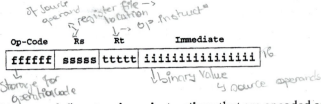

of source operand → register file location   *→ op instruct?*

Op-Code	Rs	Rt	Immediate
ffffff	sssss	ttttt	iiiiiiiiiiiiiiii

Storage for operation code   *binary value*   *source operands*

The MIPS architecture defines two **jump instructions** that are encoded as follows:

Op-Code	Target
00001f	tttttttttttttttttttttttttt

26 → specify memory locat?

When these instructions are executed, they perform the equivalent of a high-level language "go to" instruction. The lower 26 bits of the instruction are used to specify a location in memory to jump to where the next instruction will be found to execute.

1.10   INSTRUCTION SET

Refer to Appendix A for a quick reference to the **MIPS instruction set** and other useful information. Appendix C provides a more detailed description of each of the integer instructions for the MIPS architecture. Note that unique binary codes are assigned to each instruction. In reviewing the list of instructions in Appendix A, you will find that the machine has instructions to add and subtract. The operands (source values) for these operations come from the register file and the results go back to the register file. When programming in assembly language we use a mnemonic to specify which operation we want the computer to perform, and we specify the register file locations using the names of the register file locations.

Let us suppose that an assembly language programmer wants to add the contents of register $a1 to the contents of register $s1, and to place the result in register $v1. The assembly language instruction to accomplish this is

```
add  $v1, $a1, $s1
```

The equivalent pseudocode statement is

```
$v1 = $a1 + $s1
```

Let us suppose that an assembly language programmer wants to subtract the contents of register $s1 from the contents of register $s0 and place the results in register $s7. The assembly language instruction to accomplish this is

```
sub $s7, $s0, $s1
```

The equivalent pseudocode statement is

```
$s7 = $s0 - $s1
```

The MIPS architecture includes logical bitwise instructions "AND", "OR", "NOR", and "Exclusive-OR". The following "immediate format" instruction will extract a copy of the least significant bit in register $a3 and place the result in register $s0 (notice that the value 1 is in the immediate field):

```
andi $s0, $a3, 1
```

There are instructions to implement **control structures**, such as

```
"if ... then ... else ..."
```

Let us suppose that if the contents of register $s6 is less than zero, in other words, negative, we want to branch to a location in the program labeled "Quit." Otherwise (else) we want to decrement the contents of register $s6. The assembly language instructions to accomplish this are as follows:

```
bltz $s6, Quit
addi $s6, $s6, -1
```

In the preceding example, the "branch if less than zero," or `bltz` instruction compares the value stored in register file location $s6 with the value in register file location $zero. If the value in $s6 is less than $zero, then the content of the PC is modified to point to the location in memory corresponding to the instruction in the assembly language program that the programmer labeled "Quit." One of the tasks performed by the assembler when an assembly language program is translated into machine language is to map symbolic memory location labels such as "Quit" to a relative physical address in memory. Notice that if the branch is not taken, then the next instruction that is executed will be the next instruction in sequence, namely, "add immediate," `addi`, where the immediate value −1 is added to $s6, in effect decrementing the contents of register $s6.

The **multiply instruction**, `mult`, multiplies two 32-bit binary values and produces a 64-bit product which is stored in two special registers named high and low. In this case, the destination for the result is implicitly understood. Register high will be loaded with the upper 32-bits of the product and register low will be loaded with the lower 32-bits of the product. To move a copy of the value in the high register to the register file we use the instruction `mfhi` and to move a copy of the value in the low register to the register file we use the instruction `mflo`. The following code segment shows how the 64-bit product of $a1 times $s1 can be moved into $v0 and $v1:

```
mult $a1, $s1
mfhi $v0
mflo $v1
```

The **divide instruction** given next divides the 32-bit binary value in register $a1 by the 32-bit value in register $s1. The **quotient** is stored in the low register and the **remainder** is stored in the high register. The following code segment shows how the quotient is moved into $v0 and the remainder is moved into $v1:

```
div $a1, $s1
mflo $v0
mfhi $v1
```

In the MIPS architecture, division by zero is undefined. If it is possible that the divisor could be zero, then it is the programmer's responsibility to test for this condition and to provide code to handle this special situation.

1.11   ADDRESSING MODES

The MIPS architecture is a **Load/Store architecture**, which means that the only instructions that access main memory are the load and store instructions. Only one **addressing mode** is implemented in the hardware. The addressing mode is referred to as **base address plus displacement**. A **load instruction** accesses a value from memory and places a copy of the value found in memory in the register file. For example, the instruction

```
lw $s1, 8($a0)
```

computes the **effective address** of the memory location to be accessed by adding together the contents of register $a0 (the **base address**) and the constant value eight (the **displacement**). A copy of the value accessed from memory at the effective address is loaded into register $s1. The equivalent pseudocode statement would be

```
$s1 = Mem[$a0 + 8]
```

The base address is always the content of one of the registers in the register file. The displacement is always a 16-bit constant. The constant value can range from $-32{,}768$ (-2^{16}) to $+32{,}764$ $(2^{16} - 4)$. In the case of the "load word" and "store word" instructions, the effective address must be a number that is a multiple of four, because every 32-bit word contains four 8-bit bytes.

The syntax of the assembly language load instruction is somewhat confusing. If someone were to write a new MIPS assembler, the following syntax would do a better job of conveying what the instruction actually does: lw $s1, [$a0+8]

The following is an example of a "store word" instruction:

```
sw $s1, 12($a0)
```

When the hardware executes this instruction it will compute the effective address of the destination memory location by adding together the contents of register $a0 and the constant value 12. A copy of the contents of register $s1 is stored in memory at the effective address. The equivalent pseudocode statement is

```
Mem[$a0 + 12] = $s1
```

From the point of view of an assembly language programmer, memory can be thought of as a very long linear array of locations where binary codes are stored. An effective address is a pointer to some location in this array. The PC is a pointer into a different portion of the array where the machine language code has been stored.

1.12   THE FETCH EXECUTE CYCLE

When we write a program in assembly language we are creating a list of instructions that we want the processor to execute to accomplish some task (an **algorithm**). As soon as we have acquired a functional model of the processor and know exactly what instructions the processor can perform, then we will have mastered the first necessary component to becoming a MIPS assembly language programmer.

After a programmer has written a program in assembly language using a text editor, a utility program called an assembler translates the **mnemonic** representation of each instruction to its binary representation, called **machine language**. The assembler stores the machine language code in a file on disk. To execute the program, another utility program, called a **linking loader**, loads and links together all of the necessary machine language modules into the computer's main memory, and the PC is loaded with the address of the first instruction in the main program. The last instruction executed in the user program must return control back to the operating system. This is accomplished by executing a system call that generates a software exception.

The following is a step-by-step description of the sequence of operations that must take place within a MIPS processor to fetch and execute any of the register format instructions:

1. **Instruction Fetch Phase**. An instruction is fetched from memory at the location specified by the PC. The instruction is loaded into the IR. PC is incremented by four.
2. **Operand Fetch Phase.** Two 5-bit codes, Rs and Rt, within the instruction specify which register file locations are accessed to obtain two 32-bit source operands. Decode the Op-Code.
3. **Execute Phase**. The two 32-bit source operands are routed to the ALU inputs where some operation is performed depending upon the Op-Code in the instruction.
4. **Write Back Phase.** The result of the operation is placed into the register file at a location specified by the 5-bit Rd code in the IR. Go to step 1.

EXERCISES

1.1 Explain the difference between a register and the ALU.

1.2 Explain the difference between assembly language and machine language.

1.3 Explain the difference between cache memory and the register file.

1.4 Explain the difference between the IR and the PC.

1.5 Explain the difference between a bus and a control line.

1.6 Identify a kitchen appliance that contains a control unit that issues control signals.

1.7 What is an algorithm?

1.8 Provide a step-by-step description of the sequence of operations that must take place within a MIPS processor to fetch and execute the "load word" instruction.

1.9 Provide a step-by-step description of the sequence of operations that must take place within a MIPS processor to fetch and execute the "store word" instruction.

CHAPTER 2

Algorithm Development in Pseudocode

Where does satisfaction come from?
A satisfactory.

2.1   INTRODUCTION

Experienced programmers develop their algorithms using high-level programming constructs such as the following:

- **If** (condition) **do** {this block of code} **else do** {that block of code};
- **While** (condition) **do** {this block of code};
- **For** (t0=1; t0<s0; t0++) **do** {this block of code};

The key to making MIPS assembly language programming easy is to initially develop the algorithm using a high-level **pseudocode** notation with which we are already familiar. Then in the final phase we translate these high-level pseudocode expressions into MIPS assembly language. In other words, in the final phase we are performing the same function that a compiler performs, which is to translate high-level code into the equivalent assembly language code.

2.2   DEVELOP THE ALGORITHM IN PSEUDOCODE

When documenting an algorithm in a language such as C, C++, or Java, programmers use descriptive variable names such as speed, volume, size, count, amount, etc. After the program is compiled, these variable names correspond to memory locations, and the values stored in these memory locations correspond to the values of these variables. A compiler will attempt to develop code in such a way as to keep the variables that are referenced most often in **processor registers**, because access to a variable in a processor register is faster than access to random access memory (RAM). MIPS has 32 processor registers whose names were listed in Table 1.1. In the case of the MIPS architecture, all of the data manipulation instructions and the control instructions require that their operands be in the register file.

A MIPS assembly language programmer must specify within each instruction which processor registers are going to be utilized. For example, we may have a value in register $t0 corresponding to speed, a value in register $t1 corresponding to volume, a value in register $t2 corresponding to size, and a value in register $t3 corresponding to count. When using pseudocode to document an assembly language program, we must use the names of the registers we intend to use in the assembly language code. It is advisable to create a cross-reference table that defines what each processor register is being used for within the algorithm (e.g., $t0: Sum, $v0: Count). We use register names in pseudocode so that the translation to assembly language code will be fairly simple and because we want documentation that describes how the features of the MIPS architecture are used to implement the algorithm. By documenting the values in each register at each step of the algorithm it will be a relatively simple task to derive the corresponding assembly language code. Also, the high-level documentation should be helpful in debugging a program. Pseudocode for assembly language programs should have the appearance of a high-level language in terms of control structures and arithmetic expressions.

You have probably already deduced that the **syntax** for MIPS assembly language instructions is

```
[label:] Op-Code [operand], [operand], [operand] [#comment]
```

The **label** field is optional. The operands in brackets indicate optional fields depending on the operation. The specific syntax for each instruction is shown in Appendix A. With tab(s) or space(s) separating the individual fields, the commas are optional. It is considered a good programming practice to place labels on blank lines, in which case the label is associated with the instruction on the following line. In MIPS assembly language, anything on a line following the pound sign (#) is a comment.

2.3   REGISTER USAGE CONVENTION

Within the register file, different sets of registers have been given names to remind the programmer of a **convention**, which all MIPS assembly language programmers are expected to abide by. If all the members of a programming team do not adhere to the same convention, the entire effort will result in disaster. In most real-world circumstances programmers will use functions written by other programmers whose code has been placed in a library. Any code placed in a library must adhere to the register usage convention. Students using this textbook are expected to adhere to the same convention. *Programs should run correctly, even if class members randomly exchange a function that has been specified for any particular programming assignment.*

Programs of any complexity typically involve a main program that calls functions. Any important variables in the main program that must be maintained across function calls should be assigned to registers $s0 through $s7, the **save registers**. As programs become more complex, functions will call other functions. This is referred to as **nested function calls**. For example, a programmer writing a binary search function would first call a sort function before actually implementing the binary search algorithm. A function that does not call another function is referred to as a **leaf function**. When writing a function, the programmer may utilize registers $t0 through $t9 (the **temporary registers**) with the understanding that no other code modules except values in these registers will be maintained. If additional registers are needed within the function, the programmer may use **save registers** if he or she first saves the current values on the stack and restores their values before exiting the function. Registers $s0 through $s7 are referred to as **callee-saved** registers. Registers $t0 through $t9 are referred to as **caller-saved** registers. This means that if the code module requires that the contents of certain "t" registers must be maintained upon return from a call to another function, it is the responsibility of the calling module to save these values on the stack and restore the values upon returning from the function call. Registers $a0 through $a3 are used to pass arguments to functions, and registers $v0 and $v1 are used to return values from functions. These conventions are explained in more detail in Chapter 6.

2.4   TRANSLATION OF ARITHMETIC EXPRESSIONS

In the following pseudocode arithmetic expression, what fundamental geometry formula comes to mind? **$s0=srt($a0 * $a0 +$a1*$a1)**

Let us consider a translation of this pseudocode arithmetic expression to MIPS assembly language. In this case, we are assuming that there is a library function srt which we can call that will return in $v0 the square root of the argument passed to the function in $a0. We are assuming that the results of all computations do not exceed 32 bits. (You may want to review Section 1.10 for an explanation of the multiply instruction.) The **jump and link** instruction is used to call a function. When the jump and link (jal srt) instruction is executed, the address of the next sequential instruction, which is currently in the program counter, is stored in **return address register** $ra. Then the PC is loaded with the address of the first instruction in the square-root function. The last instruction executed in the square-root function is (jr $ra), which will cause a return to the calling program by loading register $ra into the PC. The code is as follows:

```
mult  $a0, $a0        # Square $a0
mflo  $t0             # t0 = Lower 32-bits of product
mult  $a1, $a1        # Square $a1
mflo  $t1             # t1 = Lower 32-bits of product
add   $a0, $t0, $t1   # a0 = t0 + t1
jal   srt            # Call the square-root function
move  $s0, $v0        # By convention, the result of sqr is returned
                      # in $v0
```

Here is another pseudocode expression: $s0 = π * $t8 * $t8. What fundamental geometry formula comes to mind? A translation of this pseudocode arithmetic expression to MIPS assembly language is

```
li    $t0, 314156  # Load immediate Pi scaled up by 100,000
mult  $t8, $t8     # Radius squared
mflo  $t1          # Move lower 32-bits of product in low
                   # register to $t1
mult  $t1, $t0     # Multiply by scaled Pi
mflo  $s0          # Move lower 32-bits of product in low register
                   # to $s0
li    $t1, 100000  # Load immediate scale factor of 100,000
div   $s0, $t1     # Divide by scale factor
mflo  $s0          # Truncated integer result left in $s0
```

2.5   TRANSLATION OF AN `if...then...else...` CONTROL STRUCTURE

The "`if` (condition) **then** do {this block of code} **else** do {that block of code}" control structure is probably the most widely used by programmers. Let us suppose that a programmer initially developed an algorithm containing the following pseudocode:

```
if ($t8 < 0) then
        {$s0 = 0 - $t8
        $t1 = $t1 +1}
else
        {$s0 =   $t8
        $t2 = $t2 + 1}
```

When the time comes to translate this pseudocode to MIPS assembly language, the results could appear as follows:

```
        bgez  $t8, else      # if ($t8 is greater than or equal to
                             # zero) branch to else
        sub   $s0, $zero, $t8  # $s0 gets the negative of $t8
        addi  $t1, $t1, 1    # increment $t1 by 1
        b     next           # branch around the else code

else:
        mov   $s0, $t8       # $s0 gets a copy of $t8
        addi  $t2, $t2, 1    # increment $t2 by 1
next:
```

Notice that the condition of the instruction bgez, "branch if greater than or equal to zero," is the opposite of the condition shown in the pseudocode. This reversal of the relational operator typically occurs when translating pseudocode to assembly language because the conditional branch instruction transfers control to the else code. Notice also that at the assembly language level, an explicit branch instruction must be included to branch around the else code. Finally, notice how the comments in the code help to make the connection back to the original pseudocode.

2.6 TRANSLATION OF A while CONTROL STRUCTURE

Another control structure is "while (condition) do {this block of code}".

Let us suppose that a programmer initially developed a function described by the following pseudocode:

```
while ($a1 < $a2) do
    {$a1 = $a1 + 1
     $a2 = $a2 - 1}
```

The following is a translation of the while pseudocode into MIPS assembly language:

```
while:
        bgeu    $a1, $a2, done   # If( $a1 >= $a2) Branch to done
        addi    $a1, $a1, 1      # $a1 = $a1 + 1
        addi    $a2, $a2, -1     # $a2 = $a2 - 1
        b       while            # Branch to while
done:
```

Notice the reversal of the relational operator in the assembly language code.

2.7 TRANSLATION OF A for LOOP CONTROL STRUCTURE

A **for loop control structure** is very useful. Let us suppose that a programmer initially developed an algorithm containing the following pseudocode:

```
$a0 = 0;
for ( $t0 =10; $t0 > 0; $t0 = $t0 -1) do
        {$a0 = $a0 + $t0}
```

In one sentence, can you describe what this algorithm accomplishes?

The following is a translation of the preceding **for** loop pseudocode to MIPS assembly language:

```
        li      $a0, 0          # $a0 = 0
        li      $t0, 10         # Initialize loop counter to 10
loop:
        add     $a0, $a0, $t0
        addi    $t0, $t0, -1    # Decrement loop counter
        bgtz    $t0, loop       # If ($t0 > 0) Branch to loop
```

2.8   TRANSLATION OF A switch CONTROL STRUCTURE

Following this paragraph, you will find a pseudocode example of a **switch control structure** wherein the binary value in register $s0 is shifted left either one, two, or three places depending upon what value is read in. You will learn in Chapter 3 that shifting a binary number left one bit position is equivalent to multiplying the number by two, and that shifting the number left two bit positions is equivalent to multiplying by four, etc. Here is the pseudocode:

```
      $s0 = 32;
top:  cout << "Input a value from 1 to 3"
      cin >> $v0
      switch($v0)
            {case(1):{$s0 = $s0 << 1; break;}
             case(2):{$s0 = $s0 << 2; break;}
             case(3):{$s0 = $s0 << 3; break;}
             default:  goto top; }
      cout << $s0
```

The following is a translation of the switch pseudocode into MIPS assembly language:

```
            .data
            .align   2
jumptable: .word    top, case1, case2, case3
prompt:     .asciiz  "\n\n Input a value from one to three:"
            .text
top:
            li       $v0, 4         # Code to print a string
            la       $a0, prompt
            syscall
            li       $v0, 5         # Code to read an integer
            syscall
            blez     $v0, top       # Default for less than one
            li       $t3, 3
            bgt      $v0, $t3, top  # Default for greater than three
            la       $a1, jumptable # Load address of jumptable
            sll      $t0, $v0, 2    # Compute word offset (multiply
                                    #    by four)
            add      $t1, $a1, $t0  # Form a pointer into jumptable
            lw       $t2, 0($t1)    # Load an address from jumptable
            jr       $t2            # Jump to specific case "switch"
case1:      sll      $s0, $s0, 1    # Shift left logical 1 bit
            b        output
case2:      sll      $s0, $s0, 2    # Shift left logical 2 bits
            b        output
```

```
case3:    sll     $s0, $s0, 3    # Shift left logical 3 bits

output:
          li      $v0, 1         # Code to print an integer is 1
          move    $a0, $s0       # Pass argument to system in $a0
          syscall                # Output result
```

2.9   ENCODING THE MIPS INSTRUCTION SET

When the MIPS architecture was defined, the designers decided that the machine would have instructions to perform the operations listed in Appendix C. At that time, the designers also decided on a binary operation code for each instruction, and the specific instruction format in binary. The list of instructions in Appendix C is a subset of the instructions available in most MIPS implementations. Appendix F provides a list of floating-point instructions.

The designers of the MIPS assembler, the program that translates MIPS assembly language code to MIPS binary machine language code, also made some decisions to simplify the task of writing MIPS assembly language code. The MIPS assembler provides a set of **macro** (also called **synthetic** or **pseudo**) **instructions**. Every time a programmer specifies a macro instruction, the assembler replaces it with a set of actual MIPS instructions to accomplish the task. Appendix D provides a list of macro instructions. For example, let us suppose a programmer used the absolute value macro instruction:

```
          abs    $s0, $t8
```

The MIPS assembler would then insert the following three instructions to accomplish the task:

```
          addu   $s0, $zero , $t8
          bgez   $t8, positive
          sub    $s0, $zero, $t8
positive:
```

Using the macro instructions simplifies the task of writing assembly language code, and programmers are encouraged to use the macro instructions. Note that when there is a need to calculate time and space parameters for a code module the abs macro instruction would correspond to three clock cycles to execute (worse case), and three memory locations of storage space. The macro instructions have been placed in a separate appendix (Appendix D) to assist the programmer in recognizing these two classes of instructions.

2.10   ASSEMBLER DIRECTIVES

A list of **assembler directives** appears in Appendix A. Looking back at the example assembly language code for the switch control structure you will see some of these assembler directives. Assembler directives give a programmer the ability to establish some initial data structures that will be accessed by the computer at "run time" when the machine language code corresponding to the assembly language code in the text segment is executed. The **text segment** is identified by the assembler directive .text. All assembler directives can be identified by the fact that they begin with a period symbol. The computer does not execute these assembler directives at run time. The assembler directives simply direct the assembler to establish some data structures before run time. For example, to allocate space in memory for a one-dimensional array of 1024 integers, the next construct is used in the C language:

```
int ARRAY[1024] ;
```

In MIPS assembly language, the corresponding construct is

```
        .data
ARRAY:  .space 4096
```

The assembler directive .data tells the assembler that all following data allocation directives should allocate data in a portion of memory called the **data segment**. Notice that the assembler directive .space requires that the amount of space allocated must be specified in bytes. Since there are 4 bytes in a word, an array of 1024 words is an array of 4096 bytes. In assembly language, this data structure is accessed using the associated name that appears in the label field.

To **initialize a memory array** before program execution begins with a set of 16 values corresponding to the powers of 2 (2^N with N going from 0 to 15), the following construct is used in the C language:

```
int  Pof2[16] ={1, 2, 4, 8, 16, 32, 64, 128, 256, 512, 1024,
               2048,4096, 8192, 16384, 32768}
```

In MIPS assembly language the corresponding construct is

```
        .data
Pof2:   .word 1, 2, 4, 8, 16, 32, 64, 128, 256, 512, 1024, 2048,
              4096, 8192, 16384, 32768
```

The terminology used to describe the specific elements of an array is the same as that used in high-level languages: Element zero "Pof2[0]" contains the value one (1). Element one "Pof2[1]" contains the value 2, etc.

Here is an example of how MIPS code can be written to access element two in the array and place a copy of the value in register $s0:

```
la    $a0,  Pof2        # a0 = &Pof2
lw    $s0,  8($a0)      # s0 = MEM[a0 + 8]
```

Observe that the **load address** (`la`) macro instruction is used to initialize a pointer in $a0 with the base address of the array labeled "Pof2."

After executing the **load word** (`lw`) instruction, register $s0 will contain the value 4. To access specific words within the array, the constant offset must be some multiple of four. The smallest element of information that can be accessed from memory is a byte, which is 8 bits of information. There are 4 bytes in a word. The address of a word is the same as the address of the first byte in a word. The following instruction will access the last word in the Pof2 array, and the binary value corresponding to 32,768 will be loaded into $s0:

```
lw    $s0,  60($a0)     # s0 = MEM[a0 + 60]
```

Additional assembler directives will be described in due course.

2.11   INPUT AND OUTPUT

The MIPS simulator PCSpim, which is described in Chapter 4, provides a set of **system services** to perform input and output. At the end of Appendix A you will find a table describing all the system services. At the pseudocode level, it is sufficient to indicate input and output using any construct you are familiar with. C++ programmers should be comfortable with the following constructs:

```
To output a string: cout << "Please input a value for N";
To input a decimal value from the keyboard:    cin >> v0;
To output a value in decimal representation:    cout << a0;
```

We will close this chapter with a complete MIPS assembly language example. Let us suppose we want to write an interactive MIPS assembly language program to find the sum of the integers from 1 to N, where N is a value read in from the keyboard. In other words, we wish to do the following: $1 + 2 + 3 + 4 + 5 + 6 + \ldots + N$.

Highlighted next is a pseudocode description of the algorithm and the corresponding assembly language program, where $t0 is used to accumulate the sum, and $v0 is used as a loop counter that starts with the input value N and counts down to 1. In reality this program computes the sum of the integers in reverse order. Computing the sum in reverse order results in a slightly more efficient program.

MIPSter is a free text editor specifically designed for MIPS assembly language programmers. It can be downloaded from

```
http://www.downcastsystems.com/mipster.asp
```

It is suggested that you use the MIPSter editor to create a copy of the following program and experiment with the different features of the MIPS simulator (all MIPS assembly language source code files must be saved as text only):

```
###################################################################
#     Program Name: Sum of Integers
#     Programmer:  YOUR NAME
#     Date last modified:
###################################################################
# Functional Description:
# A program to find the sum of the integers from 1 to N, where N is
#     a value
# read in from the keyboard.
###################################################################
# Pseudocode description of algorithm:
# main:   cout << "\n Please input a value for N = "
#         cin >> v0
#         If ( v0 > 0 )
#                 {t0 = 0;
#                 While (v0 > 0 ) do
#                         {t0 = t0 + v0;
#                         v0 = v0 - 1}
#                 cout << "   The sum of the integers from 1 to N
#                               is ", t0;
#
#                 go to main
#                 }
#         else
#                 cout << "\n  **** Adios Amigo - Have a good
#                               day ****"
###################################################################
# Cross References:
# v0: N,
# t0: Sum
###################################################################
          .data
Prompt: .asciiz    "\n  Please Input a value for N =  "
Result: .asciiz    "The sum of the integers from 1 to N is"
Bye:     .asciiz    "\n **** Adios Amigo - Have a good day****"
          .globl    main
          .text
main:
          li        $v0, 4       # system call code for Print String
          la        $a0, Prompt  # load address of prompt into $a0
          syscall                # print the prompt message
          li        $v0, 5       # system call code for Read Integer
          syscall                # reads the value of N into $v0
          blez      $v0, End     # branch to end if  $v0  < = 0
          li        $t0, 0       # clear register $t0 to 0
```

```
Loop:
        add       $t0, $t0, $v0    # sum of integers in register $t0
        addi      $v0, $v0, -1     # summing integers in reverse order
        bnez      $v0, Loop        # branch to loop if $v0 is != 0

        li        $v0, 4           # system call code for Print String
        la        $a0, Result      # load address of message into $a0
        syscall                    # print the string

        li        $v0, 1           # system call code for Print Integer
        move      $a0, $t0         # move value to be printed to $a0
        syscall                    # print sum of integers
        b         main             # branch to main

End:    li        $v0, 4           # system call code for Print String
        la        $a0, Bye         # load address of msg. into $a0
        syscall                    # print the string
        li        $v0, 10          # terminate program run and
        syscall                    # return control to  system
```

MUST HAVE A BLANK LINE AT THE END OF THE TEXT FILE

To call the system service to print a string, three assembly language instructions must be executed. The first three instructions in the above program accomplish this task. The value four (4) is loaded into $v0 to specify Print String system service. (li $v0, 4). The **symbolic address** of the memory location where a string of characters has been stored in memory must be loaded into $a0. (la $a0, Prompt) In other words, $a0 is a pointer to the string. The instruction syscall causes a transfer of control to some assembly code that prints a string of characters to the console. When the system service has accomplished its task, control is returned to the user program where the instruction following the syscall is executed.

This is a good time to introduce the assembler directive, .asciiz. This directive is used to initialize memory with a string of ASCII codes corresponding to the characters that are enclosed within quote marks following this assembler directive. The ASCII codes are shown in Appendix B. Each ASCII binary code consists of 8 bits, a byte. This assembler directive will place a **null character (NUL) code**, which is zero, into memory at the end of the string of character codes. In the example program shown above, the second instruction initializes a pointer to the first character code in a string stored in memory. The symbolic label associated with this memory location is "Prompt". The Print String system service will continue to print all the characters found in memory following the first character code until it finds the NUL, at which time it then returns control to the user program. The NUL serves as a stop sign to the Print String system service.

The assembler directive .ascii does *not* place a NUL code at the end of the string. If you want the system service to print many lines of text, then all but the last line of text that appears in your source code should be initialized using the .ascii directive.

To call the system service to **read an integer** from the keyboard, only two assembly language instructions must be executed. The next two instructions in the program provide an example. The value 5 must be loaded into $v0. (li $v0, 5) The instruction syscall causes a transfer of control to some assembly code, which responds to every keystroke on the keyboard. When the "enter" key is depressed, control is returned to the user program where the instruction following the syscall is executed. The binary equivalent of the decimal integer typed in will be returned to the user in $v0.

Calling the system service to **print the decimal** equivalent of a binary number involves three instructions, as shown in the following example:

```
li      $v0, 1    # system call code for Print Integer
move    $a0, $t0  # move value to be printed to $a0
syscall           # print sum of integers
```

The value 1 must be loaded into $v0. The value to be printed must be moved into $a0. The instruction syscall causes a transfer of control to some assembly code, which performs the conversion from the binary representation to a decimal representation and prints the corresponding string of decimal characters to the console, left justified.

The following example shows how to call the system service to **read in a string** of characters from the keyboard:

```
li      $v0, 8        # system call code Read String
la      $a0, Buffer   # $a0 is a pointer to an input buffer
li      $a1, 60       # specifies the maximum length of input buffer
syscall               # read a string and store it into the buffer
```

The value 8 must be loaded into $v0. The address of the input buffer must be loaded into $a0. The maximum buffer length must be loaded into $a1. An assembler directive must appear somewhere within the source code to **allocate space** for the buffer in the memory data segment. For example, the following directive will do the job:

```
Buffer:    .space 60
```

EXERCISES

2.1 Using Appendix A, translate each of the following pseudocode expressions into MIPS assembly language:

(a) t3 = t4 + t5 - t6;

(b) s3 = t2 / (s1 - 54321);

(c) sp = sp - 16;

    (d) `cout << t3;`

    (e) `cin  >> t0;`

    (f) `a0 = &array;`

    (g) `t8 = Mem(a0);`

    (h) `Mem(a0+ 16) = 32768;`

    (i) `cout  << "Hello World";`

    (j) `If (t0 < 0) then t7 = 0 - t0 else t7 = t0;`

    (k) `while ( t0 != 0) { s1 = s1 + t0; t2 = t2 + 4; t0 = Mem(t2) };`

    (l) `for ( t1 = 99; t1 > 0; t1=t1 -1)  v0 = v0 + t1;`

  (m) `t0 = 2147483647 - 2147483648;`

    (n) `s0 = -1 * s0;`

    (o) `s1 = s1 * a0;`

    (p) `s2 = srt(s0² +   56) / a3;`

    (q) `s3 = s1 - s2 / s3;`

    (r) `s4 = s4 * 8;`

    (s) `s5 = 7 * s5;`

2.2 Analyze the assembly language code that you developed for each of the above pseudocode expressions and calculate the number of clock cycles required to fetch and execute the code corresponding to each expression. Assume it takes one clock cycle to fetch and execute every instruction except multiply, which requires 32 clock cycles, and divide, which requires 38 clock cycles.

2.3 Show how the following expression can be *evaluated* in MIPS assembly language, without modifying the contents of the "s" registers:

    `[$t0=($s1-$s0/$s2)*$s4;`

2.4 Show how the following pseudocode expression can be *efficiently* evaluated in MIPS assembly language:

    `$t0=$s0/8-2*$s1+$s2;`

Number Systems

Where do you find the trees in Minnesota?
Between da twos and da fours.

3.1   INTRODUCTION

The decimal number system uses 10 different digits (symbols), $(0, 1, 2, 3, 4, 5, 6, 7, 8, 9)$. The **binary number system** uses only two digits, 0 and 1, which are represented by two different voltage levels within a computer's electrical circuits. Any value can be represented in either number system as long as there is no limit on the number of digits we can use. In this chapter, we will provide a method for converting values in one number system to another. We will also discuss the process of binary addition and subtraction, and how to detect if overflow occurred when performing these operations.

3.2   POSITIONAL NOTATION

No doubt, the reason we use the decimal number system is that we have 10 fingers. Possibly, for primitive cultures it was sufficient to communicate a quantity by holding up a corresponding number of fingers between 1 and 10, and associating a unique sound or symbol with these 10 quantities.

The Babylonians used written symbols for numbers for thousands of years before they invented the zero symbol. The zero symbol is the essential component that makes it possible to use the positional number system to represent an unlimited range of integer quantities. When we express some quantity such as 2056 in the decimal number system, we interpret this to mean $2 * 1000 + 0 * 100 + 5 * 10 + 6 * 1$.

The **polynomial representation** of 2056 in the base 10 number system is

$$N = 2 * 10^3 + 0 * 10^2 + 5 * 10^1 + 6 * 10^0$$

Let us assume that aliens visit us from another galaxy where they have evolved with only eight fingers. If these aliens were to communicate the quantity 2056 in the base 8 number system (**octal**), how would you find the equivalent value as a decimal number? The method is to evaluate the polynomial

$$N = 2 * 8^3 + 0 * 8^2 + 5 * 8^1 + 6 * 8^0$$

Upon evaluation, we obtain

$$N = 2 * 512 + 0 * 64 + 5 * 8 + 6 = 1070$$

Therefore, 2056 in the base 8 number system is equivalent to 1070 in the base 10 number system. Notice that these aliens would only use eight different symbols for their eight different digits. These symbols might be $(0,1,2,3,4,5,6,7)$, or they might be some other set of symbols such as $(\Omega, \sqrt{}, \Sigma, \beta, \partial, \&, \$, \%)$; initially, the aliens would have to define their digit symbols by holding up an equivalent number of fingers.

3.3   CONVERTING BINARY NUMBERS TO DECIMAL NUMBERS

Polynomial expansion is the key to converting a number in any alien number system to the decimal number system. The binary number system may be an alien number system as far as you are concerned, but you now possess the skill to convert any binary number to the equivalent decimal value. As an exercise, convert the binary number 011010 to a decimal number. We have

$$N = 0 * 2^5 + 1 * 2^4 + 1 * 2^3 + 0 * 2^2 + 1 * 2^1 + 0 * 2^0$$

Memorizing the following powers of two is an essential component of mastering this number conversion process:

2^0	2^1	2^2	2^3	2^4	2^5	2^6	2^7	2^8	2^9	2^{10}
1	2	4	8	16	32	64	128	256	512	1024

$$N = 0 * 32 + 1 * 16 + 1 * 8 + 0 * 4 + 1 * 2 + 0 * 1$$

Therefore, the binary number 011010 is equivalent to 26 in the decimal number system.

3.4   DETECTING WHETHER A BINARY NUMBER IS ODD OR EVEN

Given any binary number, there is a simple way to determine whether the number is **odd or even**. If the rightmost digit in a binary number is a one, then the number is odd. For example 00011100 is an even number, which is the value 28 in the decimal number system. The value 0001001 is an odd number—specifically, the value 9 in decimal.

When writing MIPS assembly code the most efficient method for determining if a number is odd or even is to extract the rightmost digit using the logical AND instruction followed by a branch-on-zero instruction. This method requires only two clock cycles of computer time to accomplish the task. The use of division to determine if a number is odd or even is *very* inefficient because it can take as many as 38 clock cycles for the hardware to execute the division instruction.

The following segment of MIPS assembly language code adds one to register $s1 only if the contents of register $s0 is an odd number:

```
        andi    $t8,    $s0, 1    # Extract the Least Significant Bit (LSB)
        beqz    $t8     even      # If LSB is a zero, Branch to even
        addi    $s1,    $s1, 1    # Increment count in s1
even:
```

3.5 MULTIPLICATION BY CONSTANTS THAT ARE A POWER OF TWO

Another important feature of the binary number system is that multiplication by two may be accomplished by shifting the number left one bit. Multiplication by four can be accomplished by shifting left two bits. In general, multiplication by any number that is a power of two can be accomplished in one clock cycle using a shift left instruction. For some implementations of the MIPS architecture, it takes 32 clock cycles to execute the multiply instruction, but it takes only one clock cycle to execute a shift instruction. Let us suppose that the following pseudocode describes a desired operation:

```
$v1 = $t3 * 32
```

The most efficient way to execute this is a shift left logical by 5 bits.

```
sll     $v1, $t3, 5    # $v1 = $t3 << 5
```

Notice that the constant 5 specifies the shift amount, and you should recall that

$$2^5 = 32$$

Let us suppose that the original value in register $t3 is the binary number 0000000000011010. This pattern of binary digits shifted left five bits is 0000001101000000. The value in $t3 is equivalent to 26 in the decimal number system. After shifting the binary number left five bits we have a binary number that is equivalent to 832 in the decimal number system (26 * 32). The analogous situation in the decimal number system is multiplication by ten. Taking any decimal number and shifting it left one digit is equivalent to multiplication by ten.

3.6 THE DOUBLE-AND-ADD METHOD

A quick and efficient method for converting binary numbers to decimal involves scanning the binary number from left to right, starting with the leftmost 1. As you scan to the right, double the value accumulated so far, and if the next digit to the right is a 1, add 1 to your accumulating sum. In a previous example, we had the binary number 00011010, which is equivalent to 26 decimal. Let's use the **double-and-add** method to convert from binary to decimal:

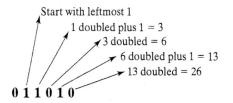

3.7   CONVERTING DECIMAL NUMBERS TO BINARY NUMBERS

A simple procedure to convert any **decimal numbers to binary** follows. Essentially, this procedure is the inverse of the double-and-add process explained in the preceding section. The process involves repeatedly dividing the decimal number by two and recording the quotient and the remainder. After each division by two, the remainder is the next digit in the binary representation of the number. Recall that any time an odd number is divided by two the remainder is one. So the remainder obtained after performing the first division by two corresponds to the least significant digit (LSD) in the binary number. The remainder after performing the second division is the next more significant digit in the binary number. The following example illustrates the procedure:

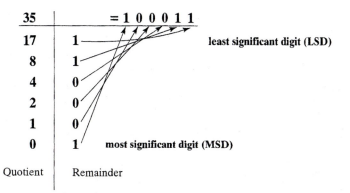

3.8   THE TWO'S COMPLEMENT NUMBER SYSTEM

Up to this point, there has been no mention of how to represent **negative binary numbers**. With the decimal number system, we commonly use a plus or minus sign and a magnitude. We do *not* use a sign magnitude representation for binary numbers. For binary numbers, we use the **signed two's complement number system**, sometimes referred to as the radix complement. The major benefit of the two's complement number system is that it simplifies the design of the hardware to perform addition and subtraction. Numbers represented in the two's complement number system have a straightforward polynomial expansion. For example, an 8-bit binary number would be evaluated with the use of the following polynomial expansion:

$$N = -d_7 * 2^7 + d_6 * 2^6 + d_5 * 2^5 + \ldots. + d_1 * 2^1 + d_0$$

In the two's complement number system, all numbers that have a one in the most significant digit (MSD) are negative numbers. The most significant digit has a *negative* weight associated with it. In the two's complement number system, the value positive 1 as an 8-bit number is 00000001 and negative 1 is 11111111. Evaluate the polynomial to verify this assertion.

3.9   THE TWO'S COMPLEMENT OPERATION

When we take the two's complement of a number, the result will be the negative of the original value. One method of performing the two's complement operation is to complement all of the digits in the binary representation and then add one to this new binary value.

For example, take the value 26, which as an 8-bit binary number is 00011010. What does the value negative twenty-six (-26) look like in the two's complement number system? Performing the two's complement operation on 00011010, we get 11100110. We have

Original value 26	00011010
Complement every bit	11100101
Add one (1)	+1

This is the value negative 26 11100110 in the two's complement number system.

Evaluate the polynomial to verify that this is negative 26.

3.10   A SHORTCUT FOR FINDING THE TWO'S COMPLEMENT OF ANY NUMBER

There is a simple one-step procedure that can be used to perform the two's complement operation on any number. This is the preferred procedure because it is faster and less prone to error. With this procedure, the original number is scanned from right to left, leaving all least significant zeros and the first one unchanged and then complementing the remaining digits to the left of the first one. Let's apply this procedure with an example. Suppose we start with the value negative 26. If we perform this shortcut two's complement operation on negative 26 we should get positive 26 as a result. Here is our work:

Original value -26	11100110
	Complemented
Resulting value $+26$	00011010

3.11   SIGN EXTENSION

When the MIPS processor is executing code, a number of situations arise where 8-bit and 16-bit binary numbers need to be expanded into a 32-bit representation. For values represented in the two's complement number system, this is a trivial process. The process simply involves extending a copy of the most significant bit into all of the additional significant digits. For example, the value 6 represented as an 8-bit binary number is 00000110, and the value 6 as a 32-bit binary number is 00000000000000000000000000000110.

The same rule applies for negative numbers. For example, the value negative 6 represented as an 8-bit binary number is 11111010, and the value negative 6 as a 32-bit binary number is 11111111111111111111111111111010.

3.12   BINARY ADDITION

With the two's complement number system, adding numbers is a simple process even if the two operands are of different signs. The sign of the result will be generated correctly as long as overflow does not occur. (See Section 3.14.) Simply keep in mind that if the sum of three binary digits is two or three, a carry of a one is generated into the next column to the left. In the following example, where there is a carry of a one, it is shown in a smaller type font:

	Decimal	Binary
		1 1 1
	29	00011101
	14	00001110
Sum	43	00101011

Notice how, in the third column to the left, we add one plus one and get two (10) for the result. The sum bit is a zero and the carry of one is generated into the next column. In this next column, we add the carry plus the two ones within the operands and get three (11) as a result. The sum bit is a one and the carry of one is generated into the next column.

3.13   BINARY SUBTRACTION

Computers perform subtraction by adding the two's complement of the subtrahend to the minuend. This is also the simplest method for humans to use when dealing with binary numbers. Let's take a simple 8-bit example where we subtract 26 from 35:

Minuend is 35	00100011			111 11
Subtrahend is 26	−00011010	Take two's complement and add		00100011
Difference	9			+11100110
				00001001

Notice when we add the two binary numbers together, there is a carry out. We don't care if there is carry. Carry does *not* indicate that overflow occurred. Converting the binary result to decimal, we get the value 9, which is the correct result.

3.14   OVERFLOW DETECTION

Registers within any computer consist of a finite number of bits. When performing arithmetic the possibility exists that the correct result cannot be represented with the limited number of bits that are available in the machine's registers. When this situation arises we say that **overflow** has occurred within the computer hardware.

In the two's complement number system, detection of overflow is a simple proposition. When adding numbers of opposite signs, overflow is impossible. When adding numbers of the same sign, the result must have the same sign as the operands, otherwise overflow occurred. More specifically, this is called **signed overflow**. The most important thing to remember is that a carry at the most significant stage does *not* signify that signed overflow has occurred in the two's complement representation. When two negative numbers are added together, there will always be a carry at the most significant digit, but this does *not* necessarily mean that signed overflow has occurred. The term **unsigned overflow** refers to a situation where two unsigned numbers are added together and a carry occurs at the most significant stage. In the MIPS processor, all binary addresses pointing to memory locations are interpreted as unsigned numbers (positive values only). In unsigned representation, all digits in the binary representation are interpreted as having a positive weight. You will notice that in Appendix C there are a number of instructions specifically implemented to operate on unsigned numbers. The distinction between signed and unsigned numbers is purely a function of how we wish to interpret a sequence of binary digits. If we wish to interpret the most significant digit in a binary number as having a positive weight then we are interpreting the number as an unsigned number.

In mathematics, we refer to a number line that goes to infinity in the positive and negative directions. In the case of computers, with limited precision, we do not have a number line. Instead, we have a number circle like the following:

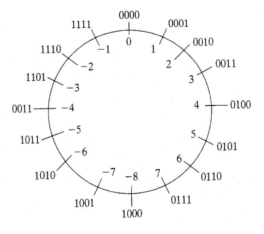

When we add 1 to the most positive value, overflow occurs, and the result is the most negative value in the two's complement number system. Let us take a very small example. Suppose we have a computer with only four bits of precision. The most positive value is 7, which is (0111) in binary. The most negative value is negative 8, which is (1000) in binary. With the two's complement number system, the range of negative values is 1 greater than the range of positive values.

3.15   HEXADECIMAL NUMBERS

Assembly language programmers very frequently use the **hexadecimal number system** because it provides a compact method for communicating binary information. The hexadecimal number system is a base 16 number system. In this case, the 16 unique symbols used as digits in hexadecimal numbers are (0, 1, 2, 3, 4, 5, 6, 7, 8, 9, A, B, C, D, E, F). A convention has been adopted to identify a hexadecimal number. The two characters 0x always precede a hexadecimal number. For example, the hexadecimal number 0x1F corresponds to the decimal value 31, and corresponds to the value 00011111 in the binary number system.

The value 16 is equal to 2^4. Converting between binary and hexadecimal representation requires no computation: it can be done by inspection. The following table is the key to making these conversions. Converting a hexadecimal number to binary simply involves replacing every hexadecimal digit with the corresponding 4-bit code in the table below. For example, 0xA2F0 in hexadecimal corresponds to 1010001011110000 in binary. To convert a binary number to hexadecimal, start with the rightmost bits and break up the binary number into groups of 4 bits each. Then, using the following table, replace every 4-bit code with the corresponding hexadecimal digit:

Decimal	Binary	Hexadecimal
0	0000	0x0
1	0001	0x1
2	0010	0x2
3	0011	0x3
4	0100	0x4
5	0101	0x5
6	0110	0x6
7	0111	0x7
8	1000	0x8
9	1001	0x9
10	1010	0xA
11	1011	0xB
12	1100	0xC
13	1101	0xD
14	1110	0xE
15	1111	0xF

For example, the 16-bit binary number 1111011011100111 is equivalent to 0xF6E7.

EXERCISES

3.1 Convert the decimal number 35 to an 8-bit binary number.

3.2 Convert the decimal number 32 to an 8-bit binary number.

3.3 Using the double-and-add method, convert 00010101 to a decimal number.

3.4 Using the double-and-add method, convert 00011001 to a decimal number.

3.5 Explain why the LSD of a binary number indicates whether the number is odd or even.

3.6 Convert the binary number 00010101 to a hexadecimal number.

3.7 Convert the binary number 00011001 to a hexadecimal number.

3.8 Convert the hexadecimal number 0x15 to a decimal number.

3.9 Convert the hexadecimal number 0x19 to a decimal number.

3.10 Convert the decimal number −35 to an 8-bit two's complement binary number.

3.11 Convert the decimal number −32 to an 8-bit two's complement binary number.

3.12 Assuming the use of the two's complement number system find the equivalent decimal values for the following 8-bit binary numbers:

    (a) 10000001
    (b) 11111111
    (c) 01010000
    (d) 11100000
    (e) 10000011

3.13 Convert the base 8 number 204 to a decimal number.

3.14 Convert the base 7 number 204 to a decimal number.

3.15 Convert the base 6 number 204 to a decimal number.

3.16 Convert the base 5 number 204 to a decimal number.

3.17 Convert the base 10 number 81 to a base 9 number.

3.18 For each row of the following table, convert the given number to each of the other two bases, assuming the two's complement number system is used:

16-Bit Binary	Hexadecimal	Decimal
1111111100111100		
	0xFF88	
		−128
1111111111111010		
	0x0011	
		−25

3.19 You are given the following two numbers in two's complement representation:

01101110
00011010

Perform the binary addition. Did signed overflow occur? Explain how you determined whether or not overflow occurred.

3.20 In this chapter, the one's complement number system was never mentioned, but at `http://courses.cs.vt.edu/csonline/NumberSystems/Lessons/` you can learn about it. Explain the major trade-offs between using the one's or two's complement system.

3.21 You are given the following two numbers in two's complement representation:

$$11101000$$
$$-00010011$$

Perform the binary subtraction. Did signed overflow occur? Explain how you determined whether or not overflow occurred.

3.22 Sign extend the two-digit hex number 0x88 to a four-digit hex number. 0x____.

3.23 The following subtract instruction is located at address 0x00012344:

```
loop:    addi    $t4, $t4, -8
         sub     $t2, $t2, $t0
         bne     $t4, $t2, loop
```

What are the two possible values for the contents of the PC register after the branch instruction has executed? 0x____ 0x____
This branch instruction is described in Appendix C.

3.24 You are given the following two 8-bit binary numbers in the two's complement number system:

$$X = \underline{10010100}_2 = \underline{}_{10} \qquad Y = \underline{00101100}_2 = \underline{}_{10}$$

What values do these numbers represent in decimal? Perform the following arithmetic operations on X and Y:

$$
\begin{array}{ccc}
X + Y & X - Y & Y - X \\
10010100 & 10010100 & 00101100 \\
00101100 & &
\end{array}
$$

Show your answers as 8-bit binary numbers in the two's complement number system. To subtract Y from X, find the two's complement of Y and add it to X. Indicate whether overflow occurs in performing any of these operations.

Now show a solution to the same arithmetic problems using the hexadecimal representations of X and Y.

3.25 The following code segment is stored in memory starting at memory location 0x00012344:

```
loop:    lw      $t0, 0($a0)    #
         addi    $a0, $a0, 4    #
         andi    $t1, $t0, 1    #
         beqz    $t0, loop      #
```

What are the two possible values for the contents of the PC after the branch instruction has executed? In the comments field, add a pseudocode description for each instruction.

0x_____   0x_____

CHAPTER 4

PCSpim, The MIPS Simulator

My software never has bugs.
It just develops random features.

4.1 INTRODUCTION

A simulator for the MIPS R2000/R3000 is available free of charge. It can be down-loaded from

    http://www.cs.wisc.edu/~larus/spim.html

MIPSter is a free text editor specifically designed for MIPS assembly language pro-grammers. It can be downloaded from

    http://www.downcastsystems.com/mipster.asp

There is a Unix version, and a Windows version called **PCSpim**. The name SPIM is just MIPS spelled backward. Jim Larus at the University of Wisconsin developed the initial version of SPIM in 1990. The major improvement in the latest version over previous versions is a feature to save the log file. After saving the log file, it can be opened using a text editor. Using the cut and paste tools, we can now print anything of interest relat-ed to the program that just ran. After you have downloaded PCSpim, you should re-view the accompanying "Help File." A more complete and up-to-date version of SPIM documentation is available at the following Web site:

    http://www.cs.wisc.edu/~larus/SPIM/cod-appa.pdf

This document provides a detailed explanation of the Unix version of SPIM. It is a sug-gested supplement to this textbook.

4.2 ADVANTAGES OF A SIMULATOR

There are a number of advantages to using a simulator when first learning to program in assembly language. We can learn the language without having to buy a MIPS-based computer. The simulator provides debugging features. We can single step through a program and watch the contents of the registers change as the program executes, and we can look at the contents of memory. We can set breakpoints. A programming mistake in a simulated environment will not cause the actual machine running the simulation to crash. A programming mistake in a simulated environment will usually result in a message or a simulated exception, where a trap handler will print a message to help us identify what instruction caused the exception.

This simulator does have some disadvantages. There is no linking loader phase. When developing an application to run on an actual MIPS processor we would assemble each code module separately. Then when the time comes to run the program, the loader would be used to relocate and load all the modules into memory and link them. Also this SPIM assembler/simulator does not provide a capability for users to define macros.

4.3   USING PCSPIM

Here are the steps we go through to write and run a PCSpim program: First, we use a word processor such as Notepad or **MIPSter** to create an assembly language source program file. Then we save the file as "text only" and launch PCSpim. In the **Simulator** pull-down menu check the settings, making sure that the delayed-branch and delayed-load boxes are *not* checked. In the **File** pull-down menu, select **Open** or just click the first icon on the tool bar. Select **All Files** for the **Files of type**. Figure 4.1 shows the bottom **messages** window announcing that the program has been successfully

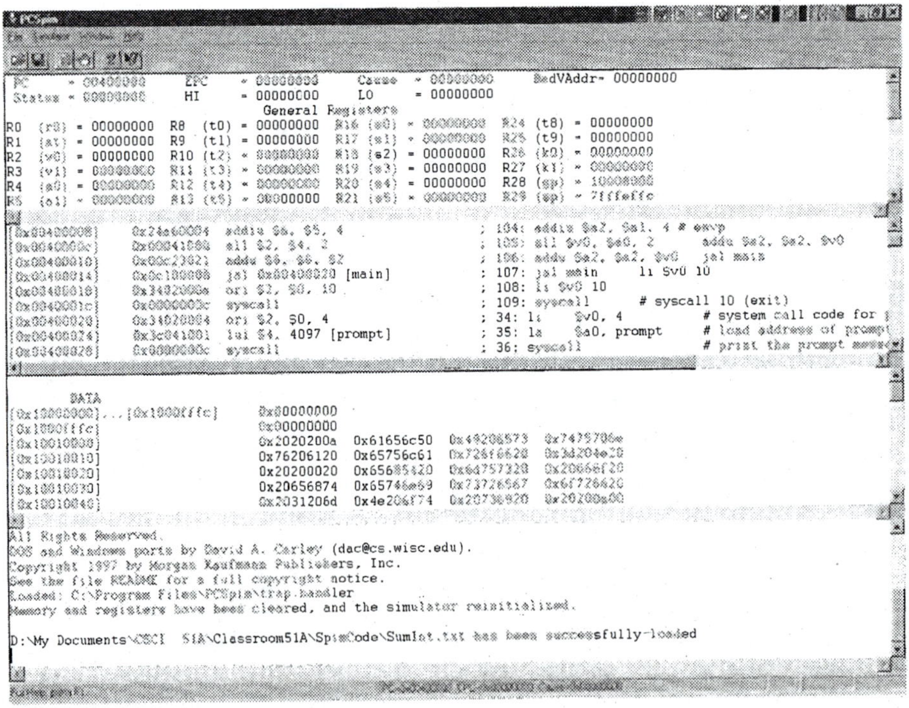

FIGURE 4.1

PCSpim messages window

loaded. Three other windows also display useful information. The **registers window**, which is the top window, displays the contents of the MIPS registers. The next window down displays the contents of the **text segment**, and the window below that displays the **data segment**. To open the **Console**, select the **Window** pull-down menu and choose **Console**.

In examining the contents of the **registers** window at the top, you will find that all the registers initially contain zero, except for the PC and the stack pointer ($sp). A short sequence of instructions in the system kernel is always executed to launch a user program. That sequence of instructions starts at address 0x00400000.

To run the program, pull down the **Simulator** menu and select **Go** or just click on the third icon in the tool bar. The program that ran for this example—Sum of Integers—is shown in Section 2.2. For this example, we ran and responded with values every time we were prompted to "Please Input a value" as shown in Figure 4.2. Analysis of the code will reveal that the program will terminate when the value 0 is typed in. When the program terminates, it would be appropriate to **Save Log File**. This can be done by clicking the second icon on the tool bar or selecting this option under the **File** pull-down menu. To run the program again, always **Reinitialize** and **Reload** the program, which are commands under the **Simulator** menu.

Entering a value for N greater than 65,535 will result in computing a sum that exceeds the range for a 32-bit binary representation. The MIPS hardware contains a circuit to detect when overflow occurs, and an exception is generated when overflow is detected. One of the commands under the **Simulation** menu is **Break**. If a program ever gets into an infinite loop, use this command to stop the simulation. Always **Reinitialize** and **Reload** the program after the program has been aborted using the **Break** command.

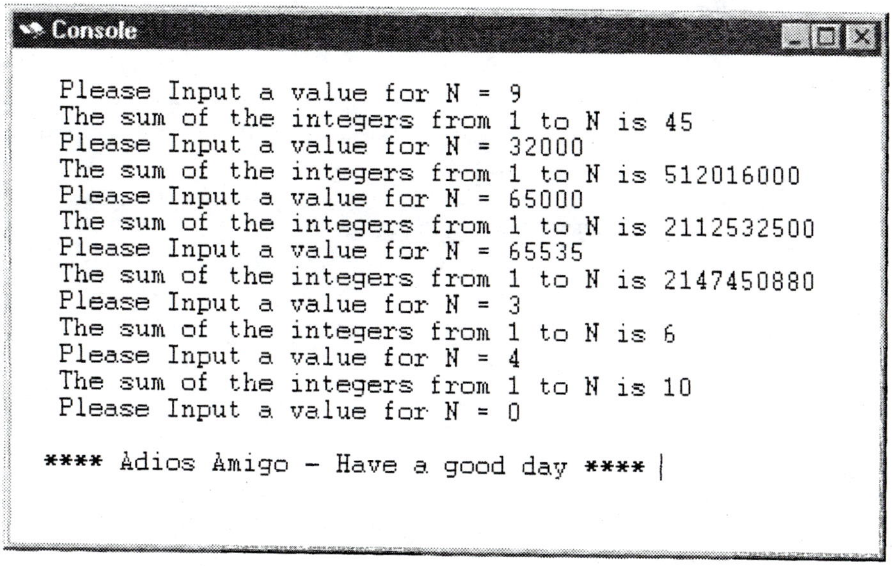

```
Console                                            _ □ ✕

   Please Input a value for N = 9
   The sum of the integers from 1 to N is 45
   Please Input a value for N = 32000
   The sum of the integers from 1 to N is 512016000
   Please Input a value for N = 65000
   The sum of the integers from 1 to N is 2112532500
   Please Input a value for N = 65535
   The sum of the integers from 1 to N is 2147450880
   Please Input a value for N = 3
   The sum of the integers from 1 to N is 6
   Please Input a value for N = 4
   The sum of the integers from 1 to N is 10
   Please Input a value for N = 0

   **** Adios Amigo - Have a good day **** |
```

FIGURE 4.2

PCSpim console window

An examination of the **Registers** window after the program has run to completion shows registers $v0 and $t0 both contain the value 10 (0x0000000a). Can you explain why? You can find out by using the **Single Step** option to run the program and to watch the contents of these registers change as each instruction is executed. In **Single Step** (function key F10) mode, the next instruction to be executed will be highlighted in the **Text Segment** window. To debug more complex programs you can set breakpoints at strategic locations within the code. In this case, you must analyze the text segment to identify the hexadecimal address where you would like to place a breakpoint. **Breakpoints** is a command under the **Simulator** menu.

4.4   ANALYZING THE TEXT SEGMENT

An examination of **text segment** that follows is especially enlightening. This text segment, taken from the log file, corresponds to the program in Section 2.2. The first column is the hexadecimal address of the memory location where each instruction was stored into memory. The second column shows how each assembly language instruction is encoded in machine language. The last column shows the original assembly language code. The code is as follows:

Address	Machine Language		Original Code	
[0x00400020]	0x34020004	ori $2, $0, 4	; 34:	li $v0, 4
[0x00400024]	0x3c041001	lui $4, 4097 [prompt]	; 35:	la $a0, prompt
[0x00400028]	0x0000000c	syscall	; 36:	syscall
[0x0040002c]	0x34020005	ori $2, $0, 5	; 38:	li $v0, 5
[0x00400030]	0x0000000c	syscall	; 39:	syscall
[0x00400034]	0x1840000d	blez $2 52 [end-0x00400034]	; 41:	blez $v0, end
[0x00400038]	0x34080000	ori $8, $0, 0	; 42:	li $t0, 0
[0x0040003c]	0x01024020	add $8, $8, $2	; 44:	add $t0, $t0, $v0
[0x00400040]	0x2042ffff	addi $2, $2, -1	; 45:	addi $v0, $v0, -1
[0x00400044]	0x14403ffe	bne $2, $0, -8 [loop-0x00400044]	; 46:	bnez $v0, end
[0x00400048]	0x34020004	ori $2, $0, 4	; 47:	li $v0, 4
[0x0040004c]	0x3c011001	lui $1, 4097 [result]	; 48:	la $a0, result
[0x00400050]	0x34240022	ori $4, $1, 34 [result]		
[0x00400054]	0x0000000c	syscall	; 49:	syscall
[0x00400058]	0x34020001	ori $2, $0, 1	; 51:	li $v0, 1
[0x0040005c]	0x00082021	addu $4, $0, $8	; 52:	move $a0, $t0
[0x00400060]	0x0000000c	syscall	; 53:	syscall
[0x00400064]	0x04013fef	bgez $0 -68 [main-0x00400064]	; 54:	b main
[0x00400068]	0x34020004	ori $2, $0, 4	; 56:	li $v0, 4
[0x0040006c]	0x3c011001	lui $1, 4097 [bye]	; 57:	la $a0, bye
[0x00400070]	0x3424004d	ori $4, $1, 77 [bye]		
[0x00400074]	0x0000000c	syscall	; 58:	syscall
[0x00400078]	0x3402000a	ori $2, $0, 10	; 60:	li $v0, 10
[0x0040007c]	0x0000000c	syscall	; 61:	syscall

The **assembler** is the program that translates assembly language instructions into machine language instructions. To appreciate what this translation process entails, every student should translate a few assembly language instructions into machine language instructions. We now demonstrate this translation process. We will be using the information in Appendix C to verify that 0x3402000a is the correct machine language encoding of the instruction `ori $2, $0, 10.`, which is the next to last instruction in the preceding text segment, located at memory location [0x00400078]. You will notice that the original code assembly language instruction was the macro instruction `li $v0, 10`. Performing an OR immediate with the constant value 10 will accomplish the objective, so this is how the assembler implements this macro instruction.

In Appendix C, we are shown how this instruction is encoded in binary:

```
ori Rt,Rs,Imm    #RF[Rt]=RF[Rs] OR Imm

Op-Code   Rs    Rt          Imm

001101sssssttttiiiiiiiiiiiiiiii
```

The macro instruction "load immediate" (`li $v0, 10`) was the original assembly language instruction. Looking in Appendix D, we find that the actual instruction (`ori $2, $0, 10`) is used to accomplish the task of loading register $v0 with the value 10. In Table 1.1, we find that register number 2 corresponds to the register with the name $v0. So now all we have to do is fill in the binary encoding for all the specified fields of the instruction. Specifically, the immediate value is 10, which is 0000000000001010, Rt is 00010, and Rs is 00000. The final step involves translating the 32-bit binary value to hexadecimal (the alternating shading is helpful for distinguishing each 4-bit field):

```
Op-Code        Rs    Rt         Imm
001101 00000 00010 0000000000001010
  3   4   0   2   0   0   0   a
```

Use the information in Appendix C to verify that 0x2042ffff is the correct machine language encoding of the instruction `addi $v0, $v0, -1`. This instruction is located at memory location [0x00400040].

4.5 ANALYZING THE DATA SEGMENT

Within the **data segment** of this example program, the following three ASCII strings were defined with the use of the assembler directive `.asciiz`:

```
        .data
prompt: .asciiz  "\n   Please Input a value for N = "
result: .asciiz  "   The sum of the integers from 1 to N is "
bye:    .asciiz  " **** Adios Amigo - Have a good day ****"
```

This directive tells the assembler to place the ASCII codes corresponding to the strings within quotes into memory sequentially one after another. Notice the z at the end of the directive. This indicates that the assembler should create a null-terminated string. The ASCII null character(NUL) is an 8-bit binary value zero (0) (See Appendix B.) The **Print String** system utility stops printing characters in a string when it finds a NUL.

Other *special characters* in strings follow the C convention:

- newline   \n
- tab   \t
- quote   \"

To begin this analysis, let's take the characters "Please". Using Appendix B, look up the ASCII code for each of the characters:

$$\textbf{P} \rightarrow 0x50 \quad \textbf{l} \rightarrow 0x6c \quad \textbf{e} \rightarrow 0x65 \quad \textbf{a} \rightarrow 0x61 \quad \textbf{s} \rightarrow 0x73 \quad \textbf{e} \rightarrow 0x65$$

The operating system has allocated space in memory for our data segment to begin at address 0x10010000. Locating this ASCII code sequence is an interesting exercise, complicated by the fact that Intel processors store characters within words in reverse order, and PCSpim is running on an Intel-based platform. We have highlighted the location of these characters within the following data segment of memory:

		a e l P		e s	
[0x10010000]	0x2020200a	0x**61656c50**	0x49206**573**	0x7475706e
[0x10010010]	0x76206120	0x65756c61	0x726f6620	0x3d204e20
[0x10010020]	0x20200020	0x65685420	0x6d757320	0x20666f20
[0x10010030]	0x20656874	0x65746e69	0x73726567	0x6f726620
[0x10010040]	0x2031206d	0x4e206f74	0x20736920	0x20200a00

Can you find the null character that terminates the first string?

4.6   SYSTEM I/O (INPUT/OUTPUT)

The developers of the SPIM simulator wrote simple decimal input/output functions. Access to these functions is accomplished by generating a software exception. The MIPS instruction a programmer uses to invoke a software exception is syscall. There are 10 different services provided. In your programs, you specify what service you want to perform by loading register $v0 with a value from 1 to 10. The following table describes each **system service**:

Service	Code in $v0	Argument(s)	Result(s)
Print Integer	1	$a0 = number to be printed	
Print Float	2	$f12 = number to be printed	
Print Double	3	$f12 = number to be printed	
Print String	4	$a0 = address of string in memory	
Read Integer	5		number returned in $v0
Read Float	6		number returned in $f0
Read Double	7		number returned in $f0
Read String	8	$a0 = address of input buffer in memory $a1 = length of buffer (n)	
Sbrk	9	$a0 = amount	address in $v0
Exit	10		

4.7   DEFICIENCIES OF THE SYSTEM I/O SERVICES

These simple I/O functions provided by the developers of SPIM have some undesirable characteristics:

- The decimal output function prints left justified. In most situations we would rather see the numbers printed right justified.
- The decimal input function always returns some value even if the series of keystrokes from the keyboard does not correctly represent a decimal number. You can verify this by running the following program and typing the following strings, each of which does not correctly represent a decimal integer value or the value exceeds the range that can be represented as a 32-bit binary value:

```
2.9999999
1  9
3A
4-2
-4+2
ABCD
2,147,463,647
2147463648
-2,147,463,648
-2147463649
```

```
          .data
prompt:   .asciiz  "\n    Please Input a value"
bye:      .asciiz  "\n    **** Adios Amigo - Have a good day *****"
          .globl   main
          .text
main:
          li       $v0, 4         # system call code for Print String
          la       $a0, prompt    # load address of prompt into $a0
          syscall                 # print the prompt message
          li       $v0, 5         # system call code for Read Integer
          syscall                 # reads the value into $v0
          beqz     $v0, end       # branch to end if $v0 equals 0
          move     $a0, $v0
          li       $v0, 1         # system call code for Print Integer
          syscall                 # print
          b        main           # branch to main
end:      li       $v0, 4         # system call code for Print String
          la       $a0, bye       # load address of msg. into $a0
          syscall                 # print the string

          li       $v0, 10        # terminate program run and
          syscall                 # return control to system
```

EXERCISES

4.1 Translate the following assembly language instructions to their corresponding machine language codes as they would be represented in hexadecimal (*Hint*: Refer to Appendix C and Appendix D):

```
loop:    addu      $a0, $0, $t0
         ori       $v0, $0, 4
         syscall
         addi      $t0, $t0, -1
         bnez      $t0, loop
         andi      $s0, $s7, 0xffc0
         or        $a0, $t7, $s0
         sb        $a0, 4($s6)
         srl       $s7, $s7, 4
```

4.2 What is the character string corresponding to the following ASCII codes?
0x2a2a2a2a 0x69644120 0x4120736f 0x6f67696d 0x48202d20 0x20657661
(*Hint*: Remember that for simulations running on Intel-based platforms, the characters are stored in reverse order within each word.)

4.3 Use the following program to estimate the instruction execution rate for PCSpim running on your computer (you may have to adjust the "time factor"):

```
###########################################################
# Reports elapsed time every 5 seconds over a period of one minute.
###########################################################
            .data                         # Data declaration section
msg:        .asciiz     "\n Elapsed Time = "
            .text
main:                                      # Start of code section
            li          $s1, 0            # Time counter
countdown:
            li          $s0, 2500000      # Adjustable time factor
waitloop:
            addi        $s0, $s0, -1
            bnez        $s0, waitloop
            addi        $s1, $s1, 5
            li          $v0, 4            # Print message
            la          $a0, msg
            syscall
            move        $a0, $s1
            li          $v0, 1
            syscall                       # Print amount
            addi        $t0, $s1, -60
            bnez        $t0, countdown
            li          $v0, 10
syscall
```

C H A P T E R   5

Efficient Algorithm Development

How would you describe Al Gore playing the drums?
Algorithm.

5.1 INTRODUCTION

Everyone knows exercise is the key to developing stronger muscles and muscle tone. Some students pay a good deal of money for sport club memberships, just so they can use the exercise equipment. The remaining chapters of this textbook provide a wealth of exercises students can use to strengthen their "mental muscle." Challenging yourself with these exercises is essential to becoming an efficient, productive assembly language programmer. Discussion and collaboration with your peers can be a valuable component in strengthening your mental muscle.

Students using this textbook will be presented with many challenging assembly language programming exercises. It is suggested each student should initially attempt to individually develop a pseudocode solution to each exercise. Next, the students should show each other their pseudocode, and discuss ways to refine their algorithms to make them more efficient in terms of **space and time.**

The final step is to translate the pseudocode into assembly language code, and to calculate performance indexes for their solutions. The two performance indexes are

  a. The number of words of assembly language code (space).
  b. The number of clock cycles required to execute the code (time).

5.2 INSTRUCTIONS THAT PERFORM LOGICAL OPERATIONS

The **logical operators** implemented as MIPS instructions are AND, NOR, OR, and EXCLUSIVE-OR (XOR). These instructions are extremely useful for manipulating, extracting, and inserting specifically selected bits within a 32-bit word. Programmers who really understand these instructions have a significant advantage in developing a program with superior performance. For those unfamiliar with these bitwise logical operators, the following truth table defines each of the operators:

Input x	0	0	1	1
Input y	0	1	0	1
x AND y	0	0	0	1
x OR y	0	1	1	1
x NOR y	1	0	0	0
x XOR y	0	1	1	0

In the table, x and y represent two Boolean variables, and the results of each logical operator appear in the corresponding column. These logical operations are performed upon the corresponding bits in two source registers, with each containing 32 bits, and the resulting 32 bits are stored in a destination register. The truth table describes four possible combinations of two variables, and defines the corresponding results produced by the logical operators.

Looking at the truth table for the AND operation, we find the only case where we get a 1 for a result is when x *and* y are both 1. For the OR operation, we get a 1 for a result when either x *or* y is a 1. The operator NOR stands for NOT-OR, and we notice the row in the truth table that defines the NOR operation is simply the complement of the row describing the OR operation. For the EXCLUSIVE-OR, we get 1 in the result only when the x and y input variables are different.

We will refer to the least significant bit (LSB) in a word as bit 0, and we will refer to the most significant bit (MSB) as bit 31. Note that if a logical operator has a 16-bit immediate operand, the hardware automatically zero extends the immediate value to form a 32-bit operand. One of the operands for a logical operator is usually referred to as a **mask**. The bit pattern within a mask is used to select which fields within the other register we wish to manipulate, or from which we wish to extract information. For these examples, assume that the following masks are stored in registers $t8, and $t9:

$t8 = 0xffffffc0 = 11111111111111111111111111111111111111111111111111000000

$t9 = 0x0000003f = 00000000000000000000000000000000000000000000000000111111

To move a copy of $t0 into $t1 with the lower 6 bits cleared, the instruction to accomplish this would be

```
and     $t1, $t0, $t8           # $t1 = $t0 & $t8
```

In this case, anywhere there is a 0 in the mask, we get 0 in $t0, and anywhere there is a 1 in the mask, we get a copy of $t0 in $t1.

To move a copy of $t0 into $t1 with the lower 6 bits set to 1, the instruction to accomplish this is

```
or      $t1, $t0, $t9           # $t1 = $t0 | $t9
```

In this case, anywhere there is a 1 in the mask, we get a 1 in $t1, and anywhere there is a 0 in the mask, we get a copy of $t0 in $t1.

Suppose we want to **complement** the lower 6 bits of register $t0, but leave all the other bits unchanged. The instruction to accomplish this is

```
xor     $t0, $t0, $t9          # $t1 = $t0 ^ $t9
```

Anywhere there is a 1 in the mask, we get a complement of the original value in $t0. Anywhere there is a 0 in the mask, we get a copy of the corresponding bits in $t0.

Suppose we want to know if the values in two registers $s0 and $s1 have the same sign. The instructions to accomplish this are

```
xor     $t0, $s0, $s1          # The most significant bit (MSB)
                               # of $t0 will be
                               # set to a "1" if $s0 and
                               # $s1 have different signs
bgez    $t0, same_sign         # Branch if MSD of $t0 is a zero
```

Suppose we want to swap the contents of registers $s0 and $s1. The instructions to accomplish this could be

```
xor     $t0, $s0, $s1    # Determine which bits are different
move    $s0, $s1         # Move a copy of s1 into s0
xor     $s1, $s0, $t0    # Get a copy of s0 but complement those bits
                         # that were different
```

5.3   INSTRUCTIONS THAT PERFORM SHIFT OPERATIONS

The MIPS architecture has instructions to **shift** the bits in a register either right or left. The shift left logical (sll) instruction shifts in zeros. In the case of the shift right, there is a shift right *logical* (srl) instruction, and a shift right *arithmetic* (sra) instruction. In the case of the shift right arithmetic, a copy of the most significant bit is always maintained and shifted right to ensure the sign of the number does not change. Logical shifts always shift in zeros.

Suppose $a0 contains the value −32 (11111111111111111111111111100000) and we want to divide $a0 by four. Shifting $a0 right arithmetic 2 bits will accomplish the task. The result is −8 (11111111111111111111111111111000). Note that 2^2 is equal to 4. So in the case of dividing by a value that is some power of 2, division can be accomplished in one clock cycle with the SRA instruction. In the case of odd negative numbers, this is not a truncated division. Instead, it rounds down to the next more negative integer number. For example, take the binary value equivalent to −9 and do an arithmetic shift right by one bit and the result will be −5. If truncated division of an odd negative number is required, it can still be accomplished with the following instructions:

```
sub $a0, $0, $a0    # Complement the number to make it positive
sra $a0, $a0, 1     # Shift Right by 1 is Equivalent to dividing by 2
sub $a0, $0, $a0    # Complement the number back to negative
```

Macro instructions are provided to **rotate** the bits in a register either right or left. (See Appendix D.) With these instructions, any bits shifted out of one end of the register will be shifted into the other end of the register. These macro instructions require at least 3 clock cycles to execute.

5.4 MODULAR PROGRAM DESIGN AND DOCUMENTATION

The importance of good program design and **documentation** cannot be stressed too much. Good documentation is valuable for student programmers as well as professional programmers. Over time, it is not unusual for the functional requirements of a code module to change, which will require modifications to previously written code. Often, the programmer assigned the task of modifying a code module is not the same person who created the original version. Good documentation saves hours of programmer time analyzing how existing code accomplishes its functions, and expedites the necessary modifications to the code. Every organization will have its own documentation standards. The pages that follow provide a suggested minimal documentation standard. The main components of this documentation standard are as follows:

- Functional Description
- Algorithmic Description
- Register Usage Table
- Inline Documentation

A **functional description** will provide the information anyone needs to know if they are searching for a function that would be useful is solving some larger programming problem. The functional description describes only *what* the function does, not *how* it is done. The functional description must explain how arguments are passed to the function and how results are returned (if any). The following are example functional descriptions for the classical I/O functions that are described in more detail later in this chapter:

```
Hexout($a0: value)
A 32-bit binary value is passed to the function in register $a0 and
the hexadecimal equivalent is printed out right justified.
```

```
Decout($a0: value)
A 32-bit binary value is passed to the function in register $a0 and
the decimal equivalent is printed out right justified.
```

Decin($v0: value, $v1: status)
Reads a string of decimal digits from the keyboard and returns the
32-bit binary equivalent in register $v0. If the string does not
correctly represent a decimal number error status value "1" is
returned in register $v1 otherwise the status value returned is "0"
for a valid decimal number.

Hexin (&string, value):
Scans a string of ASCII characters representing a hexadecimal number
and returns the 32-bit binary equivalent value on the stack at
Mem($sp+4). A pointer to the string is passed to the function on the
stack at Mem($sp). Upon return the pointer in (Mem$sp) will be pointing to the byte that follows the last hexadecimal digit in the string.

Pseudocode explains *how* the function is implemented. Anyone assigned the task of modifying the code will be extremely interested in the logical structure of the existing code. The logical structure of the code is more readily understood using a high-level notation. The use of high-level pseudocode is valuable during the initial development of a code module and will be especially helpful to the maintenance programmer. The original programmer usually is not the individual who will be making modifications or improvements to the code as the years pass. Pseudocode facilitates collaboration in group projects. Pseudocode facilitates debugging. Therefore, pseudocode should be a part of the documentation of every assembly language program.

When we develop code in a high-level language, the use of descriptive variable names is extremely valuable for documentation purposes. In the case of the MIPS architecture, all of the data manipulation instructions and the control instructions require that their operands be in the register file. A MIPS assembly language programmer must specify within each instruction which processor registers are going to be utilized. For example, we may have a value in register $t2 corresponding to size, and a value in register $t3 corresponding to count. When using pseudocode to document an assembly language program, we must use the names of the registers we intend to use in the assembly language code. We use register names in the pseudocode so that the translation to assembly language code will be an easy process to perform and because we want documentation that describes how the MIPS architecture actually executes the algorithm. Unless we identify the registers being used, the pseudocode is quite limited in terms of deriving the corresponding assembly language program or documenting the assembly language code.

The use of a **cross-reference table** that defines what each processor register is being used for within the algorithm will bridge the gap between a descriptive variable name and the corresponding MIPS register (for example: $t2 = Size, $t3 = Count). Shown next is an example **header** for a main program that can be used for programming assignments. Notice that the header has a register usage cross-reference table:

```
################### Example Main Program Header ##################
# Program # 1 : <descriptive name>  Programmer : < your name>
#  Due Date     : mm dd, 2002        Course: CSCI 51a
# Last Modified : mm dd hh:mm         Section:
##################################################################
#  Overall Program Functional Description:
#
##################################################################
#  Register Usage in Main:
#      s0 = Address of ...
#      s4 = value of ...
##################################################################
#  Pseudocode Description:
#
##################################################################
```

Each MIPS function should be immediately preceded by a header such as the following one, for a function:

```
#################### Example Function Header  ####################
# Function Name:
# Last Modified : month day hour: minute
##################################################################
#  Functional Description:
#
##################################################################
#  Explain what parameters are passed to the function, and how:
#      $a0 = Pointer to a string in memory
#
#  Explain what values are returned by the function, and how:
#      $v0 = Binary value returned on the stack
#      $v1 = Status value returned on the stack
#                   0 = successful, otherwise error
#
#  Example Calling Sequence :
#      <show moves of parameters to registers or the stack>
#      jal  xxxxxx
#      <returns here with . . .
##################################################################
#  Register Usage in Function:
#      t0 = Address of ...
#      t4 = value of ...
##################################################################
#  Algorithmic Description in Pseudocode:
#
##################################################################
```

The use of **in-line documentation** can be quite helpful in identifying what each block of assembly language code is accomplishing. Throughout this textbook, there are a multitude of examples of in-line documentation. The purpose of the in-line documentation is to provide a phrase that describes what is logically being accomplished, as in the following example:

```
        andi    $t8,  $s0, 1    # Extract the least significant
                                # bit (LSB)
        beqz    $t8   even      # If LSB is a zero branch to even
        addi    $s1,  $s1, 1    # Increment the odd count in $s1
even:
```

On the next three pages you will find a complete program consisting of a main program and a function module. Using the documentation, you should be able to follow the logic of what is being accomplished and how it's being accomplished. Here is the program:

```
################### Example Main Program Header ###################
# Program # 1   : <descriptive name>  Programmer : < your name>
#  Due Date     : mm dd, 2001         Course: XYZ
# Last Modified : mm dd hh:mm          Section:
###################################################################
#  Overall Program Functional Description:
#  This main line program is used to test the function "Sum."
#  After calling the function, results are printed.
###################################################################
#  Register Usage in Main:
#       $a0: used to pass the address of an array to the function
#       $a1: used to pass the length parameter "N" to the function
###################################################################
#  Pseudocode Description:
#
###################################################################
                .data
array:          .word    -4, 5, 8, -1
msg1:           .asciiz  "\n The sum of the positive values = "
msg2:           .asciiz  "\n The sum of the negative values = "
                .globl   main
                .text
main:
                li      $v0, 4     # system call code for Print String
                la      $a0, msg1  # load address of msg1 into $a0
                syscall            # print the string

                la      $a0, array # Initialize address Parameter
```

```
        li      $a1, 4        # Initialize length Parameter
        jal     Sum           # Call sum function

        move    $a0, $v0      # Sum of positive returned in $v0
        li      $v0, 1        # system call code for Print Integer
        syscall               # print the sum of positive values

        li      $v0, 4        # system call code for Print String
        la      $a0, msg2     # load address of msg2. into $a0
        syscall               # print the string

        li      $v0, 1        # system call code for Print Integer
        move    $a0, $v1      # sum of negative returned in $v1
        syscall               # print sum of negative values

        li      $v0, 10       # terminate program run and
        syscall               # return control to  system
```

```
#################### Example Function Header  ####################
# Function Name: Sum(&X, N, SP, SN)
# Last Modified : month day hour: minute
##################################################################
# Functional Description:
# This function will find the sum of the positive values SP and
# and the sum of the negative values SN in an array of words X of
# length N.
##################################################################
# "X" is the address of an array passed to the function in $a0.
# "N" is the length of the array passed to the function in $a1.
# The function returns two values:
#       (1) Sum of the positive elements SP passed back in $v0.
#       (2) Sum of the negative elements SN passed back in $v1.
#
##################################################################
#   Example Calling Sequence :
#     la    $a0, array
#     li    $a1, 4
#     jal   sum
#     move  $a0, $v0
#
##################################################################
#   Register Usage in Function:
#       a0 = address pointer into the array
#       a1 = loop counter (counts down to zero)
#       t0 = a value read from the array in memory
#       v0 = return sum of positive values
#       v1 = return sum of negative values
```

```
######################################################
#  Algorithmic Description in Pseudocode:
#        v0 = 0;
#        v1 = 0;
#        while( a1 > 0 )do
#             {
#                  a1 = a1 - 1;
#                  t0 = Mem(a0);
#                  a0 = a0 + 4;
#                  If (t0 > 0) then
#                            v0 =v0 + t0;
#                  else
#                            v1 = v1 + t0;
#             }
#        Return
######################################################
Sum:     li     $v0, 0
         li     $v1, 0            # Initialize v0 and v1 to zero
Loop:
         blez   $a1, Return       # If (a1 <= 0) Branch to Return
         addi   $a1, $a1, -1      # Decrement loop count
         lw     $t0, 0($a0)       # Get a value from the array
         addi   $a0, $a0, 4       # Increment array pointer to next word
         blez   $t0, Negative     # If value is negative Branch to negg
         add    $v0, $v0, $t0     # Add to the positive sum
         b      Loop              # Branch back for another iteration
Negative:
         add    $v1, $v1, $t0     # Add to the negative sum
         b      loop              # Branch back for another iteration
Return: jr     $ra              # Return
```

5.5   A FUNCTION TO PRINT VALUES IN HEXADECIMAL REPRESENTATION

To display anything on the monitor, the ASCII codes for the desired characters first must be placed into an array of bytes in memory (an output buffer), and then one uses a system call to print the string (syscall 4). The instructions used to print a string are as follows:

```
li       $v0, 4        # System call code for print a string
la       $a0, buffer   # Load address of  output buffer into $a0
syscall
```

The syscall will send a string of characters to the display starting at the memory location symbolically referred to by buffer. The string must contain a null character (0x00) to indicate where the string ends. It is the programmer's responsibility to place the null character at the proper location in memory to indicate where the string ends.

Notice that this particular syscall has two parameters passed to it. The value 4 passed to the system in register $v0 indicates that the programmer wants to invoke a print-string system service. The value in register $a0 is the address of the memory location where the first character of the string is located.

Since there is no system service to print values in hexadecimal representation, it would appear this should be one of the first functions we should develop. The logical instructions and the shift instruction come in handy for this algorithm. Recall that a 32-bit binary number can be represented with eight hexadecimal digits. Conceptually, then we need to iterate eight times. With each iteration, we extract the lower four bits from the binary number and then shift the binary number to the right by four bits. We examine the 4 bits that were extracted, and if the value is less than 10, we add the appropriate bias to create the corresponding ASCII code. If the value is 10 or greater, then a different bias must be added to obtain the appropriate ASCII code for the correct hexadecimal digit in the range from A through F. Once the ASCII code has been computed, it must be placed into the output buffer, starting at the rightmost digit position and working to the left. After the eight ASCII characters have been placed in the buffer, it is necessary to place three additional characters at the beginning of the buffer: specifically, the ASCII code for a space (0x20), the ASCII code for a zero (0x30), and the ASCII code for an x (0x78). Finally the content of the buffer is printed as an ASCII string, and then a return is executed.

5.6   A FUNCTION TO READ VALUES IN HEXADECIMAL REPRESENTATION

To input characters from the keyboard, one uses a system service to read a string (syscall 8). The specific set of instructions used to read a string are as follows:

```
li        $v0, 8          # system call code for Read a String
la        $a0, buffer     # load address of  input buffer into $a0
li        $a1, 60         # Length of buffer
syscall
```

The read-string system service will monitor the keyboard and as the keys are pressed, the corresponding ASCII codes will be placed sequentially into the input buffer in memory. When the **Enter** (new-line) key is pressed, the corresponding ASCII code (0x0a) is stored in the buffer followed by the null character (0x00), and control is returned to the user program.

Notice this particular syscall has three parameters passed to it: the value 8 passed to the system in register $v0 indicates the programmer wants to invoke a read-string system service, the value in register $a0 specifies the address of the input buffer in memory, and the value in register $a1 specifies the length of the buffer. To allocate space in memory for a 60-character buffer, the following assembler directive can be used:

```
.data
buffer:        .space  60
```

Since there is no system service to read values in hexadecimal representation, this could be a valuable function to develop. In general, this algorithm involves reading in a string of characters from the keyboard into a buffer, and then scanning through the string of characters, converting each ASCII code to the corresponding 4-bit value. The process is essentially the inverse of the hexadecimal output function. When each new valid hexadecimal ASCII code is found, we shift our accumulator register left four bits and then insert the new 4-bit code into the accumulator. If more than 8 hexadecimal digits are found in the input string, the number is invalid, and status information should be returned to indicate an error condition. Any invalid characters in the string, such as "G", also would be an error condition. A properly specified hexadecimal number should be preceded with the string 0x.

5.7   A FUNCTION TO PRINT DECIMAL VALUES RIGHT JUSTIFIED

We now discuss an algorithm that prints the decimal equivalent of a binary number, right justified. The input to this function is a 32-bit binary number. The output will be a string of printed characters on the monitor. When we implement this code we must determine if the input binary number is a negative value. If the number is negative, the ASCII code for a minus sign will be placed in the output buffer immediately to the left of the most significant decimal digit. The maximum number of decimal digits that will be generated is 10. The output buffer must be at least 13 characters in length. Specifically, we need a null character at the end of the buffer, possibly 10 ASCII codes for 10 decimal digits, possibly a minus sign, and at least one leading space character. For a small positive value, such as nine, there will be 11 leading space characters to ensure that the number appears right justified within a field of 12 characters.

The heart of this algorithm is a "do while" control structure. Within each iteration, we divide the number by 10. From the remainder, we derive the next ASCII code for the equivalent decimal representation. The quotient becomes the number for the next iteration. The decimal digits are derived one at a time from the least significant digit working toward the most significant digit each iteration. While the quotient is not equal to zero, we continue to iterate. When the quotient finally becomes zero, it is time to check if the number should be preceded by a minus sign, and then all remaining leading character positions are filled with the ASCII code for space. Finally, we use the system service to print the ASCII string in the output buffer.

5.8   A FUNCTION TO READ DECIMAL VALUES AND DETECT ERRORS

As we pointed out at the end of Chapter 4, the system service to read an integer has no capability of informing the user if the input string does not properly represent a decimal number. An improved integer-read function should return status information to the calling program so that the user can be prompted by the calling program to reenter the value correctly when an input error is detected.

Basically, this new input function will use syscall (8) to read a string of ASCII characters from the keyboard into a buffer, and then return the equivalent 32-bit binary integer value. If the input string can be correctly interpreted as a decimal integer, a value of zero is returned in register $v1 (the status flag). If the input string cannot be correctly interpreted, then a value of "1" is returned in register $v1. In other words, $v1 will be a flag that indicates if the input value is incorrectly specified.

This algorithm consists of three phases. In the first phase, the string is scanned looking for the first digit of the number with the possibility that the MSD may be preceded by a minus sign. The second phase involves scanning through the following string of characters, and extracting each decimal digit by subtracting out the ASCII bias. When each new decimal digit is found, we multiply our current accumulated value by 10 and add the most recently extracted decimal value to the accumulator. If overflow occurs while performing this arithmetic, then an error has occurred and appropriate status information should be returned. Detection of overflow must be accomplished by this function. An overflow exception must be avoided. Any invalid characters in the string would be an error condition. The second phase ends when a space is found or when a new-line character is found. At this time, it would be appropriate to take the two's complement of the accumulated value, if the number has been preceded by a minus sign. This can be accomplished by subtracting the accumulated value from zero. In the final phase, we scan to the end of the buffer to verify the only remaining characters in the buffer are spaces.

EXERCISES

5.1 Write a MIPS assembly language program to find the sum of the first 100 words of data in the memory data segment with the label "chico". Store the resulting sum in the next memory location beyond the end of the array "chico".

5.2 Write a MIPS assembly language program to transfer a block of 100 words starting at memory location SRC to another area of memory beginning at memory location DEST.

5.3 Write a MIPS function called ABS that accepts an integer word in register $a0 and returns its absolute value in $a0. Also, show an example code segment that calls the ABS function twice, to test the function for two different input values.

5.4 Write a function PENO (&X, N, SP, SN) that will find the sum of the positive even values and negative odd values in an array X of length N. X is the address of an array passed through $a0. N is the length of the array passed through $a1. The function should return two values:

(1) The sum of all the positive even elements in the array passed back through $v0.

(2) The sum of all the negative odd elements in the array passed back through $v1.

5.5 Write a function SUM(N) to find the sum of the integers from 1 to N, making use of the multiplication and shifting operations. The value N will be passed to the function in $a0 and the result will be returned in the $v0 register. Then write a MIPS assembly language main program that will call the SUM function five times each time passing a different value to the function for N, and then printing the results. The values for N are defined as follows:

$$N: \quad .word\ 9, 10, 32666, 32777, 654321$$

5.6 Write a function FIB(N, &array) to store the first N elements of the Fibonacci sequence into an array in memory. The value N is passed in $a0, and the address of the array is passed in register $a1. The first few numbers of the Fibonacci sequence are 1, 1, 2, 3, 5, 8, 13, ...

5.7 Write a function that will receive three integer words in registers $a0, $a1, and $a2 and will return them sorted with the minimum value in $a0 and the maximum value in $a2.

5.8 Write the complete assembly language program, including data declarations, that corresponds to the following C code fragment:

```
int main()
{       int K, Y
        int Z[50]
        Y = 56
        K = 20
        Z[K] = Y - 16 * (K/4 + 210);

}
```

Make use of the fact that multiplication and division by powers of two can be performed most efficiently by shifting.

5.9 MaxMin(&X, N, Min, Max)

Write a function to search through an array X of N words to find the minimum and maximum values. The address of the array will be passed to the function using register $a0, and the number of words in the array will be passed in register $a1. The minimum and maximum values are returned in registers $v0 and $v1, respectively.

5.10 SumMain(&X, N, Sum)

Write a function to find the sum of the main diagonal elements in a two-dimensional N-by-N array of 32-bit words. The address of the array and the size N are passed to the function in registers $a0 and $a1, respectively. The result is returned in $v0. The values in registers $a0 and $a1 should not be modified by this function. Calculate the number of clock cycles required to execute your algorithm, assuming that N = 4.

5.11 Det(&X, D)

Write a function to find the determinant of a two-by-two matrix (array). The address of the array is passed to the function in registers $a0 and the result is returned in $v0. The value in register $a0 should not be modified by this function. Calculate the number of clock cycles required to execute your algorithm.

5.12 Write a function that accepts a binary value in register $a0 and returns a value in $v0 corresponding to the number of ones in $a0.

5.13 Translate the following pseudocode expression to MIPS assembly language code:

```
        .data
zap:    .space    200
        .text

        zap[$a0] = $s0;
```

Include code to ensure that there is no array bounds violation when the sw instruction is executed. Note that the array "zap" is an array containing 50 words, thus the value in register $a0 must be in the range from 0 to 196. Include code to ensure that the value in register $a0 is a word address. If an array bounds violation is detected or the value in register $a0 is not a word address then branch to the label "Error."

5.14 Write a function to search through an array X of N words to find how many of the values are evenly divisible by four. The address of the array will be passed to the function using register $a0, and the number of words in the array will be passed in register $a1. Return the results in register $v0.

CHAPTER 6

Function Calls Using the Stack

What do you call the cabs lined up at the Dallas airport?
The yellow rows of taxis.

6.1   INTRODUCTION

One of the objectives of this textbook is to stress the fact that significant program development is a teamwork effort. Unless everyone in a programming team adheres to the same convention for passing arguments (**parameters**), the programming project will degenerate into chaos. Programmers are expected to use the convention defined in Section 6.3. If everyone uses the same convention, then it should be possible to run a main program using functions written by many different individuals.

6.2   THREE DIFFERENT MEMORY SEGMENTS

Every program has three segments of memory assigned to it by the operating system when the program is loaded into memory by the linking loader. In general, the programmer has no control over what locations are assigned, and usually the programmer does not care. There is the "text" segment where the machine language code is stored, the "data" segment where space is allocated for global constants and variables, and the **stack segment**. The stack segment is provided as an area where parameters can be passed, where local variables for functions are allocated space, and where return addresses for nested function calls and recursive functions are stored. Given this stack area in memory, it is possible to write programs with virtually no limit on the number of parameters passed. Without a stack it would be impossible to write recursive functions or reentrant functions. Reentrant functions are defined in Chapter 7. The operating system initializes register 29 ($sp) in the register file to the base address of this stack area in memory. The stack grows toward lower addresses.

6.3   ARGUMENT-PASSING CONVENTION

In addition to a register usage convention, there is a parameter-passing convention that will accommodate any number of parameters, by using the stack. This convention states that the first four "in" parameters are passed to a function in $a0, $a1, $a2, and $a3. The convention states that space will be allocated on the stack for the first four parameters even though these input values are not stored on the stack by the caller. All additional "in" parameters are passed on the stack. Register $v0 is used to return a value. Very few of the function exercises presented in this textbook involve more than four "in" parameters. Yet students need to gain some experience in passing parameter on the stack. Therefore, in all the remaining examples and exercises, students will be expected to pass all arguments on the stack even though this is not the convention.

When a programmer defines a function, the parameter list is declared. As an example, suppose the lead programmer has written the main program and he has assigned his subordinate, Jack, the task of writing a function called JACK. In the process of writing this code, it becomes clear to Jack that a portion of the task he has been assigned could be accomplished by calling a library function JILL. Let us suppose that JILL has five parameters, three of which are passed *to* the function (in parameters) and two of which are returned *from* the function (out parameters). Typically, parameters can be values or addresses (pointers). Within the pseudocode description of JILL, we would expect to find a parameter list such as JILL (A, B, C, D, E) defined.

Here is an example of how a **nested function call** is accomplished in MIPS assembly language:

```
addiu   $sp, $sp, -24    # Allocate Space on the Stack
sw      $t1,  0($sp)     # First In Parameter "A" at Mem[Sp]
sw      $t2,  4($sp)     # Second In Parameter "B" at Mem[Sp+4]
sw      $t3,  8($sp)     # Third In Parameter "C" at  Mem[Sp+8]
sw      $ra, 20($sp)     # Save Return address
jal     JILL             # Call the Function
lw      $ra, 20($sp)     # Restore Return Address to Main Program
lw      $t4, 12($sp)     # Get First Out Parameter "D"  at Mem[Sp+12]
lw      $t5, 16($sp)     # Get Second Out Parameter "E"  at Mem[Sp+16]
addiu   $sp, $sp, 24     # Deallocate Space on the Stack
```

Notice that we use the unsigned version of the add immediate instruction because we are dealing with an address, which is an unsigned binary number. We wouldn't want to generate an exception just because a computed address crosses over the midpoint of the memory space.

6.4   NESTED FUNCTION CALLS AND LEAF FUNCTIONS

The scenario described in the previous section is an example of a nested function call. When the main program called JACK (jal JACK), the return address back to the main program was saved in $ra. Before JACK calls JILL, this return address must be saved on the stack, and after returning from JILL, the return address to main must be restored to register $ra. The saving and restoring of the return address is only necessary for nested function calls. The first few instructions within the function JILL to get the input parameters A, B, and C are as follows:

```
JILL:
        lw    $a0,  0($sp)    # Get First In Parameter "A" at Mem[Sp]
        lw    $a1,  4($sp)    # Get Second In Parameter "B" at Mem[Sp+4]
        lw    $a2,  8($sp)    # Get Third In Parameter "C" at Mem[Sp+8]
```

The following are the last few instructions in the function JILL to return the two out parameters D and E:

```
        sw    $v0, 12($sp)    # First Out Parameter "D"  at Mem[Sp+12]
        sw    $v1, 16($sp)    # Second Out Parameter "E"  at Mem[Sp+16]
        jr    $ra             # Return to JACK
```

With nested function calls, sometimes there is one more complexity. Let's suppose that in the case of the function JACK it is important that the values in registers $t6 and $t7 not be lost as a result of calling JILL. The only way to ensure that these values will not be lost is to save them on the stack before calling JILL and to restore them on return from JILL. Why does Jack need to save them? Because he is calling the function JILL and JILL may use the $t6 and $t7 registers to accomplish her task. Note that an efficient programmer will save only those t registers that need to be saved. The decision as to what registers need to be saved is dependent on understanding the algorithm being implemented. A leaf function never needs to save t registers. The following is an example of how Jack would ensure that the values in registers $t6 and $t7 would not be lost:

```
        addiu $sp, $sp, -32   # Allocate More Space on the Stack <####
        sw    $t1,  0($sp)    # First In Parameter "A" at Mem[Sp]
        sw    $t2,  4($sp)    # Second In Parameter "B" at Mem[Sp+4]
        sw    $t3,  8($sp)    # Third In Parameter "C" at  Mem[Sp+ 8]
        sw    $ra, 20($sp)    # Save Return address
        sw    $t6, 24($sp)    # Save $t6 on the stack <####
        sw    $t7, 28($sp)    # Save $t7 on the stack <####
        jal   JILL            # call the Function
        lw    $t6, 24($sp)    # Restore $t6 from the stack <####
        lw    $t7, 28($sp)    # Restore $t7 from the stack <####
```

```
lw      $ra, 20($sp)    # Restore Return Address to Main Program
lw      $t4, 12($sp)    # Get First Out Parameter "D" at Mem[Sp+12]
lw      $t5, 16($sp)    # Get Second Out Parameter "E" at Mem[Sp+16]
addiu   $sp, $sp, 32    # Deallocate Space on the Stack <####
```

6.5   ALLOCATING SPACE ON THE STACK FOR LOCAL VARIABLES

As functions become more complex, a situation may arise where additional space in memory is required to accomplish a task. This could be a temporary data buffer, or a situation where the programmer has run out of registers and needs additional local variables allocated space on the stack. For example, if Jill needs a temporary array of 16 characters, the code to allocate space on the stack is the first instruction shown next. The second instruction initializes register $a0 as a pointer to the beginning of this new buffer area on the stack. The two instructions are as follows:

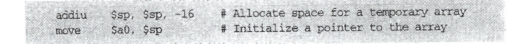
```
addiu   $sp, $sp, -16    # Allocate space for a temporary array
move    $a0, $sp         # Initialize a pointer to the array
```

Before exiting the function, this buffer space must be deallocated. For this example, deallocation is accomplished by executing the following instruction:

```
addiu   $sp, $sp, 16    # Deallocate space
```

6.6   FRAME POINTER

In the preceding code example, you will notice that allocating space on the stack for additional local variables requires the address in the stack pointer to be changed. In all previous examples we assumed the stack pointer would not change and we could reference each element on the stack with the same offset that was used by the caller. There is a way to establish a fixed reference point within each function that will maintain the same offset memory references to parameters as was used by the caller. As part of the register usage convention we have a register with the name $fp (register number 30), which stands for **frame pointer**. A stack frame is also referred to as an **activation record**. The activation record for any function is that segment in memory containing a function's parameters, saved registers, and **local variables**. When used, the frame pointer points to the top most word of the activation record. The use of a frame pointer is not a necessity. Some high-level language compilers generate code that use a frame pointer and others do not. None of the exercises in this text are sufficiently complex to warrant the use of a frame pointer.

6.7   DYNAMIC MEMORY ALLOCATION

Programs request services from the operating system by executing the `syscall` instruction, which causes a software exception. One of the functions of the operating system is to manage memory. During run time, programs can make requests to the operating system to be dynamically allocated additional space in memory by performing a `syscall` (9). The **heap** is the portion of memory managed by the operating system from which the user is allocated dynamic memory space.

The following program provides a demonstration of dynamic memory allocation with PCSpim:

```
###############################################################
# Functional Description: Testing Dynamic Storage Allocation
###############################################################
        .data           #
        .byte   -1:8    # Eight bytes sacrificed to get around bug.
msg: .asciiz "**Hello*World**"
        .text
main:                   # DYNAMICALY ALLOCATE SPACE
        li      $a0, 16 # $a0 = string length including null.
        li      $v0, 9  # Upon return $v0 will point to dynamically
        syscall         # allocated string for 16 characters.
        move    $a0, $v0 # Save Ptr to dynamically allocated string
        la      $a1, msg # $a1 = source pointer
loop:
        lb      $t9,0($a1) # Get a character.
        sb      $t9,0($v0) # Store in dynamically allocated space.
        addi    $a1, $a1, 1 # Increment pointers.
        addi    $v0, $v0, 1
        bnez    $t9, loop # Branch to loop if not at end of string.
        li      $v0, 4  # Print contents of dynamically allocated
        syscall         # string.
        li      $v0, 10
        syscall
```

The number of additional bytes of memory space requested is passed to the operating system in register $a0. A pointer to this newly allocated space is passed back to the user in register $v0. The size of the dynamic string is specified in bytes, but the number must be a multiple of four.

6.8   AN EXAMPLE DYNAMIC STRING ALLOCATION PROGRAM

The objective of the next main program and associated functions is to create two dynamic strings and then to append these two dynamic strings to create a new larger dynamic string. For this example, the first dynamic string will contain the characters This is a test and the second dynamic string will contain the characters of our string routines. Here is the code:

```
##############################################################
# Functional Description: A main program
# to test dynamic string allocation functions
# For syscall 9 - we must specify size of dynamic string
# in bytes, but the number must be a multiple of 4

##############################################################
        .data                   # Data declaration section
title:  .asciiz  "\n Dynamic Allocation of Memory Exercise\n\n"
str1:   .asciiz  "This is a test"
str2:   .asciiz  "of our string routines."
        .text
main:                           # Start of code section
        la      $a0, title
        jal     print
        la      $a0, str1
        jal     create
        move    $s1, $v0        # Get pointer to dynamic str1

        la      $a0, str2
        jal     create
        move    $s2, $v0        # Get pointer to dynamic str2
        move    $a0, $s1
        move    $a1, $s2
        jal     append
        move    $a0, $v0        # Returned pointer to new string
        jal     print
        li      $v0, 10
        syscall
##############################################################
# Functional Description: Create ($v0, $a0)
# Involves a nested call to length,
# $v0:points to a dynamically allocated string
# $a0:points to the source string that fills the dynamically
#     allocated string
##############################################################
create:
        addi    $sp, $sp,-8     # Allocate space
        sw      $ra, 0($sp)
        sw      $a0, 4($sp)     # Save source pointer
```

```
        jal     length
        addi    $a0, $v0,1      # $a0 = length N + 1
        addi    $a0, $a0,4
        srl     $a0, $a0,2
        sll     $a0, $a0,2
        li      $v0, 9
        syscall                 # $v0 now points to string with
                                # space for N+1 characters
        move    $t0, $v0        # t0 gets copy of destination pointer
        lw      $t1, 4($sp)     # Get source pointer
createloop:
        lb      $t9, 0($t1)     # Transfer character
        sb      $t9, 0($t0)
        addi    $t1, $t1, 1     # Increment temp pointers
        addi    $t0, $t0, 1
        bnez    $t9, createloop
        lw      $ra, 0($sp)
        lw      $a0, 4($sp)     # Save source pointer
        addi    $sp, $sp,8      # Deallocate space
        jr      $ra
#############################################################
# Functional Description:Length($v0, $a0) returns a value in $v0
# corresponding to the length of the string pointed to by $a0.
# Length does not enclude null at end of string

#############################################################
length:
        li      $v0, -1
        move    $t1, $a0
lengthloop:
        lb      $t0, 0($t1)
        addi    $t1, $t1, 1
        addi    $v0, $v0, 1
        bnez    $t0, lengthloop
        jr      $ra

#############################################################
# Functional Description: Append($v0, $a0, $a1)
# Involves a nested call to length. Must save $a0, $a1, & $ra
# $a0:points to first source string
# $a1:points to second source string
# $v0:points to a dynamically allocated string containing above two
# strings concatinated

#############################################################
append:
        addi    $sp, $sp,-16    # Allocate space
        sw      $ra, 0($sp)
        sw      $a0, 4($sp)     # source1 pointer
        sw      $a1, 8($sp)     # source2 pointer
```

```
              jal       length
              addi      $t3, $v0, 1    # $t3 = length first string + 1
              sw        $t3, 12($sp)   # Save on stack
              lw        $a0, 8($sp)
              jal       length         # Get length of second string
              lw        $t3, 12($sp)   # Get length of first string + 1
              add       $a0, $v0,$t3   # a0 is length of both strings + 1
              addi      $a0, $a0, 4
              srl       $a0, $a0, 2
              sll       $a0, $a0, 2
              li        $v0, 9
              syscall                  # $v0 now points to a string with
                                       # space for both strings
              move      $t3, $v0       # $t3 is temp pointer to destination
              lw        $t1, 4($sp)    # Get source 1 pointer
xferfirst:
              lb        $t9,0($t1)     # Transfer character
              sb        $t9,0($t3)
              addi      $t1, $t1, 1    # Increment temp pointers
              addi      $t3, $t3, 1
              bnez      $t9, xferfirst
              addi      $t3, $t3, -1   # To write over null char
              lw        $t2, 8($sp)    # Pointer to second string
xfersecond:
              lb        $t9,0($t2)     # Transfer character
              sb        $t9,0($t3)
              addi      $t2, $t2, 1    # Increment temp pointers
              addi      $t3, $t3, 1
              bnez      $t9, xfersecond
              lw        $ra, 0($sp)
              addi      $sp, $sp, 16 # Deallocate space
              jr        $ra
#################################################################
# Functional Description: Print($a0)Prints string pointed to by $a0
#################################################################
print:
              li        $v0, 4
              syscall
              jr        $ra
```

EXERCISES

6.1 MinMax (&X, N, Min, Max)

Write a function to search through an array X of N words to find the minimum and maximum values. The parameters &X and N are passed to the function on the stack, and the minimum and maximum values are returned on the stack. (Show how MinMax is called.)

6.2 Search (&X, N, V, L)

Write a function to sequentially search an array X of N bytes for the relative location L of a value V. The parameters &X, N, and V are passed to the function on the stack, and the relative location L (a number ranging from 1 to N) is returned on the stack. If the value V is not found, the value −1 is returned for L.

6.3 Scan (&X, N, U, L, D)

Write a function to scan an array X of N bytes, counting how many bytes are ASCII codes for

    a. uppercase letters (U)

    b. lowercase letters (L)

    c. decimal digits (D)

Return the counts on the stack. The address of the array and the number of bytes N will be passed to the function on the stack. Write a short main program to test this function.

6.4 AVA (&X, &Y, &Z, N, status)

Write a function to perform an absolute value vector addition. Use the stack to pass parameters. The parameters are the starting address of three different word arrays (vectors) : X, Y, Z, and an integer value N specifying the size of the vectors. If overflow ever occurs when executing this function, an error status of 1 should be returned and the function aborts any further processing. Otherwise, return the value 0 for status. The function will perform the vector addition

$$X_i = |Y_i| + |Z_i|, \text{with i going from 0 to N} - 1.$$

Also, write a main program to test this function.

6.5 Fibonacci (N, E)

Write an iterative function to return the Nth element in the Fibonacci sequence. A value N is passed to the function on the stack, and the Nth Fibonacci number E is returned on the stack. If N is greater than 46, overflow will occur, so return a value of 0 if N is greater than 46. Also, show an example of calling this function to return the 10th element in the sequence. The first few numbers in the Fibonacci sequence are 0, 1, 1, 2, 3, 5, ...

6.6 BubSort (&X, N)

Write a function to sort an array X of N words into ascending order using the bubble-sort algorithm. The address of the array and the value N will be passed to the function on the stack. Show how the sort function is called.

6.7 RipSort (&X, N)

Write a function to sort an array X of N words into ascending order using the ripple-sort algorithm. The address of the array and the value N will be passed to the function on the stack.

6.8 Write your most efficient assembly language code translation for the following function and main line calling program.

```
void chico (int *X, int Y, int Z)
{*X =  Y/ 4   -  Z * 10 + *X * 8 ;}
int  main()
{int J, K, L , M ;
cin >> J, K, L;
chico (& J,  K, L);
```

```
M = J  - ( K + L);
cout <<  M;
return 0
}
```

Note that all communication with the function must use a stack frame. Make use of the fact that multiplication and division by powers of 2 can be performed most efficiently by shifting.

6.9 Write a function MUL32 (m, n, p, f) that will find the 32-bit product p of two arguments m and n. If the two's complement representation of the product cannot be represented with 32 bits, then the error flag f should be set to 1 otherwise the error flag is set to 0. Pass all arguments on the stack.

6.10 The purpose of this exercise is to use pointers in assembly language to manage dynamic structures. Most modern computer languages use pointers of some kind to provide a mechanism for dealing with dynamic structures—structures whose sizes change during execution. We use syscall 9 to acquire memory space from the heap at run time. A dynamic string is a dynamically allocated varying length string. Such strings end with a null character(0). Such strings are accessed via a pointer to the first character of the string. The shortest string is defined to be of length zero, because it contains no characters other than a single null character. In this case, the pointer will point at the null character. For this exercise pointers are memory addresses passed to the functions in registers. Construct the following functions in MIPS assembly language:

Length ($v0, $a0)—returns the length in $v0 of the referenced string, pointed to by the pointer in $a0. Length is similar to the strlen function in C/C++.

Create ($v0, $a0)—returns a pointer in $v0 to the ASCII string that it dynamically allocates and loads with the string pointed to by the pointer in $a0.

Append ($v0, $a0, $a1)—returns a pointer in $v0 to the dynamic string that results from concatenating the two ASCII strings pointed to by $a0, and $a1.

Print ($a0)—prints the string pointed to by pointer in $a0.

Write a main program to test your functions by performing these actions:

1. Create a string, str1, containing "This is a test".
2. Create a string, str2, containing "of our string routines."
3. Create a string, str3, by appending str1 to str2.
4. Print a title, followed by str1, str2, and str3. Properly label your output.
5. Create an empty string; call it str4.
6. Perform a loop 5 times that

   a. Inputs a string from the keyboard, call it str5
   b. Appends str5 to str4
   c. Prints str4

C H A P T E R   7

Reentrant Functions

Why did the scientist install a knocker on his door?
To win the no-bell prize.

7.1   INTRODUCTION

It is important that all shared operating-system functions and library functions on a multitasking computer system are **reentrant**. One example of a multitasking system would be a time-sharing system. A time-sharing system is one where multiple users are sharing the computer's resources. These users are given the illusion that the computer is immediately responsive to every keystroke they make at their keyboards. In reality, every active user is given a slice of time to utilize the computer's resources. This is accomplished by having a real-time clock generator connected to the interrupt system. If the real-time clock produces an interrupt every one-hundredth of a second, then 100 completely different tasks could be running on the machine with each task running for one hundredth of a second every second. If this is a computer that executes one hundred million instructions per second, then every task could theoretically be executing nearly one million instructions per second. It may appear that 100 different tasks are running "simultaneously," but in reality each task is running for a fraction of a second every second. When the real-time clock produces an interrupt, the current address in the PC is saved in a special register called EPC, and then the PC is loaded with the address of the interrupt processing routine. To switch tasks, the current contents of all the CPU registers are saved in a block of memory devoted to the current task (the process control block), then the scheduler goes to the ready queue of waiting tasks. The highest priority task in the ready queue is selected. Using the information in the process control block for the selected task, all the CPU registers are loaded with the state that existed when this selected task was last suspended, and then the selected task begins to run.

Let's suppose that 50 users of a time-share system are all using the same compiler or text editor "simultaneously." Does this mean that 50 separate copies of the text editor must be loaded into memory, or only one copy? The answer is only one copy, if the developers of the compiler and the text editor ensured that the code was reentrant.

7.2 RULES FOR WRITING REENTRANT CODE

Reentrant code is pure code. Reentrant code has no *allocated* memory **variables** in the global data segment. It is ok to have **constants** in the global data segment, but it is not ok to have memory locations that are modified by the code in the global data segment. All local variables for reentrant code must be dynamically allocated space on the stack. Notice that dynamic allocation of memory space helps to conserve memory space, because memory is allocated space on the stack when it is needed and deallocated when it is no longer needed.

All users of a multitasking system are allocated their own area in memory for their stack. This means that if 50 different users are active, there will be 50 different stacks in different parts of memory. If these 50 different users all "simultaneously" invoke the same function, there will be 50 different areas in memory where variables are allocated space. The important concept is that there would be only one copy of the code shared by all 50 users, and when any particular user is active, the code will be operating on the data in that user's stack.

7.3 REENTRANT I/O FUNCTIONS

System services to perform I/O should be reentrant. In Chapter 5, we discussed the algorithms to perform I/O in decimal and hexadecimal representation. To make these functions reentrant, allocation of space for character buffers must be removed from the global data segment and code must be inserted into the functions to dynamically allocate space on the stack for character buffers. Let's suppose you want to allocate space on the stack for an input buffer of 32 characters, initialize a pointer in $a0 to point to the first character in this buffer, and then read in a string of characters from the keyboard into this buffer. This can be accomplished with the following instructions:

```
addiu    $sp, $sp, -32    # Allocate space on top of stack
move     $a0, $sp         # Initialize $a0 as a pointer to the buffer
li       $a1, 32          # Specify length of the buffer
li       $v0, 8           # System call code for Read String
syscall
```

7.4 PERSONAL COMPUTERS

Most personal computers now have multitasking operating systems. Normally, the O/S handles I/O services, and almost every task makes use of I/O. If I/O services are coded reentrantly, then they may be shared among the various O/S services and among various user-initiated tasks as well.

For another example, consider a situation where a text editor, a spell-check program, and voice-recognition program are all running at the same time. The voice-recognition program would be analyzing the speech waveforms producing text as input to the word processor, and the interactive spell-check monitor would be warning the user of spelling errors it detects. If all of these applications were developed by the same organization, it would have developed a library of functions to perform certain tasks. It would be important that all of the code in this library be reentrant code, because multiple applications conceivably could be executing the same library function "simultaneously."

7.5   RECURSIVE FUNCTIONS

Writing a **recursive function** is similar to writing reentrant code, with one additional complexity. In the case of reentrant code, an interrupt is the event that would create a situation where two users are sharing the same code. When an interrupt occurs, the scheduler, a system program, will save the values of all the processor registers for the suspended task into a block of memory called the process control block.

In the case of writing a recursive function, it is the responsibility of the programmer to save on the stack the contents of all registers relevant to the current invocation of the function before a recursive call is executed. Upon returning from a recursive function call the values saved on the stack must be restored to the relevant registers.

7.6   AN EXAMPLE RECURSIVE FUNCTION CALL

The quantity N factorial, or $1 * 2 * 3 * \ldots * N$, is symbolized as N!. By definition, $0! = 1$. The classical recursive definition of N! is: $N! = N * (N - 1)!$ Writing the code to evaluate N! recursively can be a mind twister. The execution of the recursive algorithm is inefficient in terms of time and space as compared to an iterative algorithm. Before every recursive call the return address must be saved on the stack. To appreciate the complexities of this recursive algorithm it is suggested that you single step through the following program:

```
#################################################################
# Functional Description: Main program to test Factorial function
# Enter a negative number to terminate run
#################################################################
        .data
prompt: .asciiz     "\n\n Give me a value for 'N': "
msg:    .asciiz     " N factorial is: "
bye:    .asciiz     " \n### Good-Bye ###"
        .text
main:   addiu       $sp, $sp, -8    # Allocate space
mloop:
        li          $v0, 4
        la          $a0, prompt
        syscall
        li          $v0, 5         # Get value for N
        syscall
        bltz        $v0, quit
        sw          $v0, 0($sp)
        jal         Fac            # Call factorial

        li          $v0, 4         # Print message
        la          $a0, msg
```

```
                syscall

                lw          $a0, 4($sp)         # Get result
                li          $v0, 1
                syscall                         # Print factorial
                b           mloop
quit:
                addiu       $sp, $sp, 8         # Deallocate space
                li          $v0, 4
                la          $a0, bye
                syscall
                li          $v0, 10
                syscall

#################################################################
# Functional Description: Recursive Factorial Fac (N: in, N!:out)
#################################################################
Fac:
                lw          $a0, 0($sp)
                bltz        $a0, Problem
                addi        $t1, $a0, -13
                bgtz        $t1, Prob           # 13 is largest value we can
                                                # accept
                addiu       $sp, $sp, -16       # Allocate
                sw          $ra, 12($sp)        # Save return address
                sw          $a0, 8($sp)
                slti        $t0, $a0, 2         # If N is 1 or 0, then return
                                                  the value 1

                beqz        $t0, Go
                li          $v0, 1
                b           facret
Go:
                addi        $a0, $a0, -1        #
                sw          $a0, 0($sp)         # Pass N-1 to factorial function
                jal         Fac                 # Recursive call
                lw          $v0, 4($sp)         # Get (N-1)! back.
                lw          $ra, 12($sp)
                lw          $a0, 8($sp)
                mult        $v0, $a0            # N*(N-1)!
                mflo        $v0
facret:
                addiu       $sp, $sp, 16        # Deallocate
                sw          $v0, 4($sp)
                jr          $ra
Problem:
                sw          $0, 4($sp)
                jr          $ra
```

7.7   MIPS MEMORY SEGMENTS

The text segment and data segments displayed by PCSpim show the addresses where the data and code are stored in memory. The following diagram provides an overall view of the entire **memory address space**:

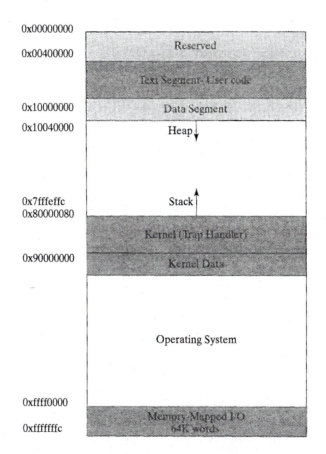

Notice that most of the upper half of the memory address space starting at 0x80000000 is reserved for the operating system. If user code ever attempts to access the space reserved for the operating system an exception will occur. This is one form of protection.

EXERCISES

7.1 Reverse

Write a reentrant function that will read in a string of characters (60 characters maximum) and will print out the string in reverse. For example the string "July is hot" will be printed as "toh si yluJ".

7.2 Palindrome (b)

Write a reentrant function that will determine if a string is a palindrome. The function should read in a string (16 characters max) placing them in a buffer on the stack. This function should call a search function to determine the exact number of actual characters in the string. A Boolean value of true or false (1 or 0) will be returned on the stack to indicate if the string is a palindrome.

7.3 Factorial

Write an iterative function to compute N factorial, and then write a recursive function to compute N factorial. Compare the time required to execute the two different versions.

7.4 Fibonacci (N, E)

Write a recursive function to return the Nth element in the Fibonacci sequence. Use the stack to pass information to and from the function. A value of 0 should be returned, if overflow occurs when this function executes.

The first few numbers in the sequence are 0, 1, 1, 2, 3, 5, 8, ...

7.5 Determinant (&M, N, R)

Write a recursive function to find the determinant of an N $\times$ N matrix (array). The address of the array M and the size N are passed to the function on the stack, and the result R is returned on the stack.

7.6 Scan (&X, Num)

Write an efficient MIPS assembly language function *Scan (&X, Num)* that will scan through a string of characters with the objective of locating where all the lower case vowels appear in the string, as well as counting how many total lower case vowels appeared in a string. Vowels are the letters a, e, i, o, and u.

The address of the string X is passed to the function on the stack, and the number of vowels found NUM is returned on the stack. A null character terminates the string. Within this function, you will call the Print Decimal function, which will be a *nested function call*. Here is an example string:

The quick brown fox.

For this example string, the output of your program would be as follows:

A Vowel was Found at Relative Position :	3
A Vowel was Found at Relative Position :	6
A Vowel was Found at Relative Position :	7
A Vowel was Found at Relative Position :	13
A Vowel was Found at Relative Position :	18

Is your Scan function a reentrant function? _____(yes/no) Explain why.

CHAPTER 8

Memory-Mapped I/O

There are three kinds of people in this world:
Those who know math and those who don't.

8.1 INTRODUCTION

Obviously, in any real computer system, the keyboard and display are outside the CPU chip. MIPS processors communicate with devices outside the CPU chip using a technique called **memory-mapped input/output** (I/O). Using memory-mapped I/O, there is no need to add any additional instructions to the MIPS instruction set. In the case of the MIPS architecture, any **load** or **store** instructions with an effective address of 0xffff0000 or greater will *not* actually access a main memory location. These addresses are reserved to make access to registers in I/O devices. These I/O device controllers must be connected to the system bus, just as the CPU is connected to the system bus, as shown in Figure 8.1. The system bus consists of a set of tiny wires laid out on a printed circuit board (motherboard) that are utilized to transmit electrical signals. Typically, the bus consists of 32 wires used to transmit address or data information, and a number of additional wires used to transmit control and status information.

Unique address decode logic is associated with each I/O register. When the MIPS processor reads from or writes to one of these addresses by placing the address on the I/O bus, the processor is actually reading from or writing to a selected register in one of the I/O device controllers. Essentially the lw and sw instructions are used to communicate with the I/O devices. Using this straightforward technique, a processor can acquire information about the state of whatever device is being controlled and can transmit signals to change the state of the device. There are many different bus standards that define different communication protocols for gaining access to the bus (**arbitration**) and for actually sending and receiving information over the bus. However, for the assembly language programmer all we really need to know is how to interpret the information in the I/O registers in order to communicate with the device.

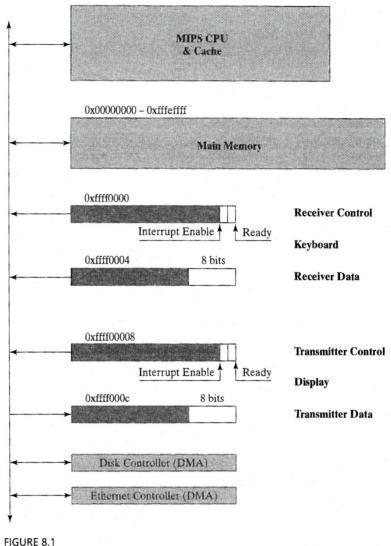

FIGURE 8.1

MIPS I/O Bus.

8.2 MEMORY-MAPPED I/O WITH PCSPIM

A feature within the PCSpim simulator provides students with a simulated version of a memory-mapped keyboard controller and a memory-mapped display controller. Anytime you write code to utilize this feature of PCSpim, you must make sure that you activate the memory-mapped I/O feature of PCSpim in the settings window before the program is loaded. If you single step through a program, while PCSpim is in this mode it will *not* respond to keystrokes from the keyboard. The best way to debug these programs is to set **breakpoints**. With PCSpim students can gain experience in writing code to communicate character by character with physical I/O devices. The code that communicates with a physical device at this level is often referred to as a **driver**. This is another significant advantage of using a simulator to learn assembly language programming. Students learning to write native assembly language code for their desktop computers, such as an Intel x86, typically never have an opportunity to write code that interfaces directly with the I/O devices. These students have to be satisfied with making calls to BIOS procedures that handle the details of communicating with the I/O devices. Typically, these students never experience the real-world challenges that arise as a result of the communication and device time delays.

The data transmission rate associated with I/O devices is much slower than the instruction execution rate of a MIPS processor. There is delay associated with transmitting signals over the system bus and there is delay associated with the physical I/O device. As you can see in Figure 8.1, there are two registers associated with the keyboard and there are two registers associated with the display. With real MIPS systems, other I/O devices such as the direct memory access (DMA) disk controller and the DMA Ethernet controller are also connected to the I/O bus, but these are *not* part of the PCSpim simulator. As controllers become more complex, more than just two registers are associated with each controller. The supplier of any device controller must provide the MIPS programmer with an explanation of how to properly use the controller registers to communicate with the I/O device. The following two sections describe how programmers communicate with the keyboard and the display via the controller registers.

8.3 COMMUNICATING WITH A KEYBOARD CONTROLLER

The two registers associated with the keyboard are called **receiver control** and **receiver data**, which are accessed by a MIPS program using the physical word addresses 0xffff0000 and 0xffff0004, respectively. To communicate with the keyboard via **polling**, we are interested in the least significant bit (the **ready bit**) of the receiver control register and the least significant 8-bits of the receiver data register. When a key is pressed on the keyboard, the 8-bit ASCII code corresponding to the symbol on the key is latched into the receiver data register and the ready bit is set to one. The following MIPS code provides an example of memory-mapped access to the **keyboard controller registers**:

```
        li      $a3, 0xffff0000 # Base Address of Memory-Mapped Terminal
CkReady:
        lw      $t1, 0($a3)     # Read from receiver control register
        andi    $t1, $t1,1      # Extract ready bit
        beqz    $t1, CkReady
        lw      $t0, 4($a3)     # Get character from keyboard
```

Notice that the first instruction loads the base address of the memory-mapped I/O area into register $a3. The rate that characters are entered at the keyboard is very slow compared to the rate that the MIPS processor can execute instructions. Typically, the MIPS processor can execute millions of instructions in the time interval between two keys being pressed on the keyboard. Notice how the three instructions in the inner loop are polling the condition of the ready bit. When the ready bit finally comes true, the ASCII code in the receiver data register is loaded into $t0 as a result of executing the lw instruction. The ready bit is cleared to zero when the keyboard controller detects the character in the receiver data register was read by the lw instruction. From this point, additional code can do whatever is necessary, such as storing the character in a buffer, and then come back to this polling code to wait for another character to be entered from the keyboard. A MIPS programmer can read only from the receiver data register and the ready bit in the receiver control register. Instructions that write to these locations will have no effect.

8.4 COMMUNICATING WITH THE DISPLAY CONTROLLER

The two registers associated with the display are called **transmitter control** and **transmitter data**, which are accessed by a MIPS programmer using the physical word addresses 0xffff0008 and 0xffff000c, respectively. To communicate with the display, we are only interested in testing the least significant bit (the ready bit) of the transmitter control register and storing an ASCII code in the least significant 8 bits of the transmitter data register. We must not store a value in the transmitter data register until the display is ready to receive it. The following MIPS code provides an example of memory-mapped access to the display controller registers:

```
        li    $a3, 0xffff0000 # Base Address of Memory-Mapped Terminal
XReady:
        lw    $t1, 8($a3)     # Read from transmitter control register
        andi  $t1, $t1, 1     # Extract ready bit
        beqz  $t1, XReady     # If not ready branch back
        sw    $t0, 12($a3)    # Send character to display
```

When the display controller detects that a character has been stored in the transmitter data register, digital logic clears the ready bit to zero. To simulate the delay inherent in communicating with a memory-mapped I/O device, PCSpim requires that a certain number of MIPS instructions be executed before the character appears in the display console and before the ready bit in the transmitter control register comes true after a character has actually been written to the transmitter data register. A MIPS programmer can write only to the transmitter data register and read only the ready bit in the transmitter control register.

8.5 A REAL-TIME CLOCK

To solve some of the homework exercises that follow, students need to determine approximately how many MIPS instructions are executed per second in this simulated PCSpim environment on their own computer. In the next program, at the label "countdown," register $s0 is loaded with a time factor of 2.5 million. There are two instructions in the "wait loop." Thus, five million instructions will be executed before leaving the "wait loop." If the program correctly reports elapsed time every 5 seconds, then we can say that the instruction execution rate is approximately one million instructions per second. Here is the program:

```
###############################################################################
# Functional Description: Reports elapsed time every 5 seconds over
# a period of one minute.
###############################################################################
        .data                       # Data declaration section
msg:    .asciiz   "\n Elapsed Time ="
        .text
main:                               # Start of code section
        li        $s1, 0
countdown:
        li        $s0, 2500000      # Time factor
waitloop:
        addi      $s0, $s0, -1      # Wait loop
        bnez      $s0, wait loop

        addi      $s1, $s1, 5
        li        $v0, 4            # Print message
        la        $a0, msg
        syscall
        move      $a0, $s1
        li        $v0, 1
        syscall                     # Print amount
        addi      $t0, $s1, -60
        bnez      $t0, countdown
        li        $v0, 10
        syscall
```

If this program does not accurately report elapsed time when running on your computer, then the "time factor" should be adjusted, and based upon this adjusted "time factor," an approximate instruction execution rate can be computed for PCSpim running on your computer.

EXERCISES

8.1 To simulate the delay inherent in communicating with a memory-mapped I/O display device, PCSpim simulates the passage of time by requiring that a certain number of instructions be executed before the ready bit in the control register (0xffff0008) comes true after a character has been written to the transmitter data register, at location 0xffff000c. Develop a program that will discover and print this delay factor for the simulated display terminal. Make sure you activate the memory-mapped I/O feature of PCSpim in the settings window before you load your program.

8.2 Using memory-mapped I/O, write a function that will perform the same task as the Print String system function. Write a main program to test this function. Make sure you activate the memory-mapped I/O feature of PCSpim in the settings window before you load your program.

8.3 Using memory-mapped I/O, write a function that will perform the same task as the Read String system function. This function will get characters from the keyboard and send them to the terminal as well as placing them in a buffer pointed to by register $a0. The contents of register $a1 specifies the length n of the buffer. It reads up to $n - 1$ characters into the buffer and terminates the string with a null byte. If fewer than $n - 1$ characters are on the current line, it reads up to and including the newline (Enter Key) and again null-terminates the string. Write a main program to test this function. Make sure that you activate the memory-mapped I/O feature of PCSpim in the settings window before you load this program.

8.4 Write a MIPS program to determine approximately how many MIPS instructions can be executed in the time that elapses between striking two separate keys on the keyboard. Your output should report what two keys were pressed and the number of MIPS instructions executed in the intervening time period. For example, if you quickly type the keys "Z" and "X" and the output "ZX 123000" appears, then you will know that the MIPS processor executed 123,000 instructions in the time interval between striking the "Z" key and striking the "X" key.

8.5 Write a MIPS program to determine the *average* number of MIPS instructions executed in the time intervals between keyboard strokes as you type a complete sentence such as "The quick brown fox jumped over the lazy dog."

8.6 This is an exercise that demonstrates a problem of performing I/O via polling where the polling rate is too slow. Write a MIPS program that polls the keyboard only once every second. If there is a character in the receiver data register, then send it to the transmitter data register for display. While the program is running, quickly type a sentence such as "The quick brown fox jumped over the lazy dog." Can you explain what appears on the display?

8.7 Real-world physical switches exhibit a phenomenon called **switch bounce**. This term refers to a situation where the binary signal coming from a switch alternates between the values 1 and 0 during a short period of time, such as one-thousandth of a second (one millisecond), before the signal becomes stable. If you would like to observe this phenomenon of mechanical forces, simply strike a hammer against a solid object and observe what happens. If input to a digital system comes from a switch that exhibits bounce, we would not want to interpret this signal as a series of ones and zeros during a short time interval such as one millisecond. For this exercise, we will say that one second of our real time represents one-thousandth of a second in simulated time. Write a MIPS program that monitors the keyboard. The first instance of a ready bit will define the beginning of a simulated one-millisecond sampling window. Striking the same key several times within this simulated one-millisecond sampling window (one second of PCSpim execution time) will represent our simulated switch bounce. Your program should transmit only one character to the display at the end of each sampling window interval, corresponding to the key that exhibited our simulated switch bounce.

CHAPTER 9

Exceptions and Interrupts

How much do pirates pay for earrings?
A buccaneer.

9.1 INTRODUCTION

Under normal circumstances, anytime the mouse button is pushed or the mouse is moved or a key on the keyboard is depressed, the computer responds. The natural question to ask is, "How does one program a computer to provide this kind of interactive response from the computer?" The answer is to provide the CPU with additional capabilities to respond to **exceptions**. Breakpoints, arithmetic overflow, traps, and interrupts are all classified as exceptions. An exception is an event that initiates a change in the normal flow of program execution. **Interrupts** are signals coming from I/O devices outside the CPU. Exception capability eliminates the need to constantly poll the keyboard and mouse. This is obviously an essential capability because if the computer were constantly polling then it would not be doing any other work. The key to building a computer system that provides superior processing throughput, and also provides an interactive response is to include within the hardware design some method for interrupting the currently running program when an exception occurs.

The method implemented by the MIPS designers to interrupt the currently running program is to include some additional hardware referred to as **Coprocessor 0** that contains a number of specialized registers that can be accessed at the assembly language level for exception handling. The top window of the PCSpim simulator displays these registers:

- EPC   Coprocessor 0 register 14 (exception program counter (EPC))
- Cause   Coprocessor 0 register 13
- BadVaddress Coprocessor 0 register 8
- Status   Coprocessor 0 register 12

The following are examples of the only two instructions available to access the coprocessor registers:

```
mfc0    $k0,    $13    # CPU register $k0 is loaded with contents of the
                       # cause register
mtc0    $0,     $12    # CPU register $0 is stored in the status register
                       # (cleared to zero)
```

The second instruction, Move to Coprocessor 0 (mtc0), is confusing because the destination register is specified in the right-hand field, differently than the way all other MIPS instructions are specified. Notice that we reference the coprocessor registers only by their numbers. They are not referenced by a name, so in-line comments are essential.

Coprocessor 0 is designed to send a signal to the CPU control unit when an exception occurs. Wires from external devices provide input interrupt signals to Coprocessor 0. Bits within the status register can be manipulated at the assembly language level to selectively enable or disable certain interrupts.

9.2   EXCEPTION CAPABILITIES OF PCSPIM

PCSpim responds to internal exceptions such as overflow and address errors. PCSpim also responds to interrupts generated by the memory-mapped keyboard or display terminal. If you single step through a program while it is in this mode it will not respond to interrupts generated from the keyboard. The best way to debug these programs is to set breakpoints. Given this feature, students now have an opportunity to experience writing code to respond to interrupts. Once again, this points out the advantage of using a simulator when learning to write assembly language code. Students learning to write native assembly language code for their desktop computers, such as an Intel x86, typically never have an opportunity to write and run interrupt handlers that enable and disable the interrupt system. Typically, these students never experience the real-world challenges that arise in writing the code that resides at the very heart of the operating system.

Most real-world embedded systems provide a **programmable timer** that will generate an interrupt after a specified period of time has elapsed. The current version of PCSpim does not include this feature. If it did, we could use such a timer to interrupt the processor every millisecond, at which time we would poll the mouse, and the keyboard for any activity. This is an alternative approach for providing interactive response without having the mouse or keyboard generating interrupts.

9.3   CPU EXCEPTION RESPONSE

Whenever an exception occurs and the MIPS processor has reached the state where the next instruction would be fetched, the CPU controller goes to a special state. In this special state, the cause register is loaded with a number to identify the source of the interrupt. Mode information in the status register is changed and all interrupts are disabled. Also, the address of the instruction that was executing when the exception occurred is saved in a register called the exception program counter (**EPC**), and the program counter is loaded with the address in memory where the first instruction of the interrupt response routine is located. If the instruction that was executing involved a memory access that caused the error, then the memory address is stored in the BadVaddress register. In the case of PCSpim, the value 64 appears in the cause register when any I/O interrupt occurs. The interrupt response routine then needs to poll all the I/O devices to determine which one generated the interrupt. The interrupt response routine is sometimes referred to as a **trap handler**.

9.4   THE TRAP HANDLER

The trap handler is simply a MIPS assembly language program, usually written by a systems programmer. The trap handler responds to the exception. In the case of the PCSpim simulator this exception processing entry point is memory location 0x8000080. This segment of memory is referred to as **kernel segment** 0 (kseg0). Students are encouraged to analyze PCSpim's trap handler, which is always displayed in the text segment. This file "trap" is available in the PCSpim folder that was downloaded over the Internet. A slightly modified version of the trap handler appears in Appendix E. To gain a more in-depth understanding of trap handlers, students will experiment by creating other modified versions of the trap handler.

The first task of the trap handler is to execute some code to save the state of the machine, as it existed right before the time when the interrupt occurred. Analyzing PCSpim's interrupt handler you will find the only registers it saves are $v0 and $a0. The interrupt handler shown in Appendix E is not reentrant because it saves these two registers in specific memory locations. To make the code reentrant these registers would have to be saved on a stack allocated to the operating system. Registers $k0 and $k1 are reserved for the operating system. This interrupt handler was written using only these registers. After the interrupt has been completely processed, the machine is placed back in its original state. When the return from exception (rfe) instruction is executed, the status register is restored its original state. The jump register (jr) instruction is used to return to the program that was interrupted.

Real-time systems and embedded processors provide much more sophisticated **priority interrupt systems**, where a lower priority interrupt handler routine can be interrupted by a higher priority interrupt. The MIPS architecture provides interrupt mask bits within the status register (bits 8 through 15), which makes it possible to write a priority interrupt handler. For our purposes, it is sufficient to enable all interrupts by setting all these bits to true, using the following instructions:

```
li      $s1, 0x0000ffff      # Mask to enable all interrupts
mtc0    $s1, $12             # Store enable bits in status register
```

9.5   ENABLING I/O INTERRUPTS

The **receiver control** (0xffff0000) register associated with the keyboard and the **transmitter control** (0xffff0008) register associated with the display each have an **interrupt enable** bit at position one (1), just to the left of the ready bit. This bit must be set to one to enable these I/O devices to generate an interrupt when the ready bit comes true. For example, the following code will enable the keyboard to generate an interrupt when a key is pressed:

```
li      $s1, 2
li      $a3, 0xffff0000    # Base address of I/O
sw      $s1, 0($a3)        # Enable keyboard interrupt
```

9.6   EXAMPLE CODE TO ENABLE INTERRUPTS

To experience the effects of an external interrupt we need a program running that gets interrupted. In the next example, we use the keyboard as a source of asynchronous interrupt signals. Using the PCSpim **Settings**, you must make sure that the modified trap handler that appears in Appendix E replaces the standard trap handler. You will notice that only five additional instructions were added to the standard trap handler to implement this special trap handler that responds to interrupts from the keyboard.

The first three instructions in the program that follows enable the keyboard to generate an exception when the ready bit comes true. (See Figure 8.1.) The next two instructions are used to enable all exceptions, including I/O interrupts. Here is the code:

```
###############################################################################
# Functional Description: Reports elapsed time every 5 seconds over
# a period of one minute. Interrupts from the keyboard are enabled.
# Must Run with Memory-Mapped I/O and the New Trap Handler in
#  Appendix E.
###############################################################################
        .data              # Data declaration section
msg:    .asciiz "\n Elapsed Time = "
        .text
main:                      # Start of code section
        li      $a3, 0xffff0000 # Base address of I/O
        li      $s1, 2
        sw      $s1, 0($a3)     # Enable keyboard interrupt
        li      $s1, 0x0000ffff # Mask to enable all exceptions
        mtc0    $s1, $12        # Store enable bits in status register
        li      $s1, 0          # Time counter
countdown:
        li      $s0, 2500000    # Time factor
```

```
waitloop:
        addi    $s0, $s0, -1
        bnez    $s0, waitloop
        bnez    $s0, waitloop    # Needed for interrupt return
        addi    $s1, $s1, 5
        li      $v0, 4           # Print message
        la      $a0, msg
        syscall
        move    $a0, $s1
        li      $v0, 1
        syscall                  # Print amount
        addi    $t0, $s1, -60
        bnez    $t0, countdown
        li      $v0, 10
        syscall
```

When this program starts running, you should start typing some sentences. There are no instructions in the above program to read a string of characters from the keyboard or to print the corresponding string, but you will notice that the interrupt handler is reading each character you type and is echoing each character back to the terminal. You are probably curious about why there are two identical branch instructions in the waitloop. The duplicate branch instruction is required because of a limitation of PCSpim. When an interrupt occurs the current instruction completes execution and the address of this instruction is saved in the EPC register of Coprocessor 0. Analyzing the current trap handler code you will discover that four is added to the value saved in the EPC and the jump register jr instruction uses this address to return to the user code. Thus, you see that the duplicate instruction is necessary to insure that the user code continues to loop until a period of five seconds have elapsed. As an experiment you can remove the duplicate branch instruction and observe the difference in behavior of the program.

An alternative solution to this problem is available. A more sophisticated version of the trap handler would analyze what type of instruction was executing when the exception occurred. If the last instruction executed were a branch or a jump, then it would *not* add four to the EPC to compute a return address. Thus, upon return the branch or jump would be reexecuted. This would be fairly simple to do because all branches and jumps have op-codes in the range from 1 to 7 in their upper six bits.

The new instructions that have been placed in the modified trap handler are shown in the next example. This code does not check the receiver ready bit since we know it is true because we received an interrupt. The transmitter ready bit is not checked because we know the display can accept characters faster than we can type characters. It would be necessary to check the transmitter ready bit if our objective is to immediately echo more than one character back to the display. With PCSpim, the cause register is loaded with the value 64 when an I/O interrupt occurs. In order to respond to I/O interrupts, the branch instruction is modified as shown:

```
        bgtz   $v0_echo            # <<<<< Modified Version ***********
```

```
################# New Code In The Trap Handler #######################
_echo:
        li     $a0, 0xffff0000     # Base address of memory-mapped devices
        lw     $v0, 4($a0)         # Get character from the keyboard
        sw     $v0, 12($a0)        # Send character to the display
        b      ret
```

9.7   A RANDOM-NUMBER GENERATOR

It's always useful to have a random-number generator, especially if you own a casino.
Some of the homework exercises will involve modifications to the following program:

```
###################################################################
# Description: Generates a random number each time key is pressed.
# Numbers range from 0 to 99. Press Enter key to quit.
# Must Run with a New Trap Handler that returns ASCII code for key
    that was pressed.
###################################################################
        .data                    # Data declaration section
nl:     .asciiz  "\n"
msg:    .asciiz  "\nHow Lucky Can You Get?"
bye:    .asciiz  "\n** Come Back Again **"
        .text
main:
        li      $a3, 0xffff0000 # Base address of I/O
        li      $s1, 2
        sw      $s1, 0($a3)     # Enable keyboard interrupt
        li      $s1, 0x0000ffff # Mask to enable all interrupts
        mtc0    $s1, $12        # Store enable bits in status register
        li      $v0, 4          # Print message
        la      $a0, msg
        syscall
        li      $t0, 211        # Seed values
        li      $t1, 3021377
clear:
        li      $v1, 0          # Clear the flag
ranloop:
        mult    $t0, $t1
        mflo    $t0
        addiu   $t0, $t0, 5923
```

```
         beqz      $v1, ranloop   # Keystroke will change $v1
                                  # to ASCII value for the key
         addiu     $v1, $v1, -10
         beqz      $v1, quit      # Quit if Enter key
         li        $v0, 4         # Print newline
         la        $a0, nl
         syscall
         li        $v1, 100       # Controls range (0-99)
         divu      $t0, $v1
         mfhi      $a0            # Get remainder
         li        $v0, 1
         syscall
         b         clear
quit:
         li        $v0, 4         # Print newline
         la        $a0, bye
         syscall
         li        $v0, 10
         syscall
```

9.8   EMBEDDED SYSTEMS REFERENCES

MIPS Technologies is the industry's leading provider of 64-bit processor architecture and cores for embedded solutions. Demand for their 64-bit technology is doubling every year. Fueling this growth is demand for features such as streaming audio and video, cryptography enhancements for e-commerce, processor clock speeds of 500 MHz in handheld devices, and the convergence of computing, communications, multimedia, and encryption.

To learn more about these applications, go to the MIPS Technologies Web site: http://www.mips.com/. An **embedded system** usually lacks secondary storage (e.g., a hard disk). Typically, all of the code is stored in read only memory (ROM). Usually, most of the code written for embedded processors is first written in a high-level language such as C. Programmers who can visualize how the high-level code will be translated into assembly language code will most likely develop the "best" code. Then programmers who have an intimate understanding of the assembly language for the target processor will analyze the code generated by the compiler looking for ways to make further optimizations. In other words, they look for ways to speed up the execution or to reduce the amount of code that has to be stored in ROM. Usually, for real-time applications, the code must be fine-tuned to meet the system's performance requirements. Any programmer with the skills to accomplish this kind of optimization will be highly sought after. The kernel of the operating system deals with responding to interrupts and scheduling tasks. This code, as well as the I/O drivers, will typically be the first code to be scrutinized. With a solid understanding of the MIPS processor and experience in developing assembly language code for the MIPS processor, it is a relatively easy task to make the transition to assembly language for other processors.

To write code for embedded systems, you will need to know more than is provided by this introductory textbook. The following three good books are targeted specifically at MIPS embedded systems programmers:

Kane, Gerry, and Heinrich, Joe. *MIPS RISC Architecture*. Upper Saddle River, NJ: Prentice Hall PTR, 1991.

Sweetman Dominic. *See MIPS Run*. San Francisco, CA: Morgan Kaufmann, 1999.

Farquhar, Erin, and Bunce, Philip. *The MIPS Programmers Handbook*. San Francisco, CA: Morgan Kaufmann, 1994.

9.9   A PROGRAMMABLE TIMER

An important feature of imbedded processors involves a programmable timer that can be used by a programmer to cause an interrupt to be generated after a specified period of time has elapsed. Two memory-mapped registers are associated with the timer: specifically, a **timer control** register and a **timer data** register. These registers could be located at addresses 0xffff0010 and 0xffff0014, respectively. The ready bit and interrupt enable bits would be located in the control register in the same relative locations that are used for the keyboard receiver control register and the display transmitter control register. (See Figure 8.1.) Writing to the timer data register would initialize an automatically decrementing counter. For PCSpim to simulate elapsed time, the counter would automatically decrement by one after a specified number of MIPS instructions have been executed. When the counter reaches zero the ready bit would come true, and if the enable interrupts bit is on, an exception would be generated. Hopefully, a future version of PCSpim will provide a simulated programmable timer.

EXERCISES

9.1 The elapsed-time program in Section 9.6 contains no instructions to read a string of characters from the keyboard or to print the corresponding string, but you notice that the modified trap handler is reading each character you type and is echoing each character back to the terminal. For this assignment, make additional modifications so that two copies of each character (e.g., aabbccdd) are echoed back.

9.2 Modify the trap handler used in the previous program so that, rather than echoing back a second copy of each character, it places an extra space between each character typed (e.g., a b c d).

9.3 Modify the trap handler used in the previous program so that every time the keyboard character is echoed back, it will follow the keyboard character with a backspace character (0x08) and a bell character (0x07). When you run this program, you will learn about a limitation of the PCSpim simulator.

9.4 The elapsed-time program contains duplicate branch instructions in the waitloop to ensure that the user code continues to loop until a period of five seconds have elapsed. Write a modified trap handler that eliminates the need for duplicate branch instructions in all programs of this type. This can be accomplished by analyzing what type of instruction was executing when the exception occurred. If the last instruction executed was a branch or a jump, then the trap handler should *not* add four to the EPC to compute a return address. Thus, upon return, the branch or jump will be reexecuted. This is fairly simple to do because all branches and jumps have op-codes in the range from 1 to 7 in their upper six bits.

9.5 Modify the trap handler associated with the elapsed-time program in Exercise 9.1 so that the first time an exception is generated from the keyboard the trap handler will ask the user to type in a password, followed by an "enter" key. The secret password will be "MIPS". Until such time that the correct password is entered, the trap handler will not return from the exception, but will keep asking for a password. As each character of the password is entered, echo back an asterisk (*). After the password has been entered once, the program should run normally, allowing the user to type messages between the elapsed-time announcements.

9.6 Random-number generators are used in all kinds of games as well as in discrete simulation packages. The desired range of values produced by the random-number generator depends on the type of event we are simulating. Write a MIPS program that will produce *truly* random numbers that are a function of *when* a key on the keyboard is pressed, and, in addition, the *range* of values produced will be a function of which key is pressed. By subtracting 38 from the ASCII code for the following keys, you will have a useful number to control the range of values produced by your generalized random-number generator:

Key	Range	Game
2	1 – 2	Coin Toss
6	1 – 6	Roll of a die
Z	1 – 52	Card Games

9.7 Modify the random-number generator so that you can play "craps" with the computer. This requires that two random numbers be computed and printed each time you press the six key.

9.8 Modify the random-number generator so that you can play card games with the computer. Assuming that we are playing with a single deck, the challenge here is to ensure that no duplicate numbers are printed and that the program stops when all 52 numbers have been produced.

9.9 As you recall, user programs are not allowed to access the area of memory where kernel data and code reside. Verify whether PCSpim simulates this security feature by writing a user program that attempts to read and write to this restricted area of memory.

9.10 Experiment with PCSpim to see if a user program can put the machine into kernel mode, and then execute some user code that accesses the restricted area of memory.

9.11 Write a user program that is designed to clear to zero all the memory locations reserved for user code.

9.12 Write a function, *Adduovf* (x, y, s), that will find the 32-bit sum s of two unsigned arguments x and y. An exception should be generated if the unsigned representation of the sum results in overflow. Perform all communication on the stack.

9.13 Write a function, *Add64*, that will perform the 64-bit addition x = y + z, where the values for x, y, and z are stored as *two* 32-bit words each:

```
Add64 (x1, x0, y1, y0, z1, z0)
```

All six parameters are passed on the stack. If the 64-bit sum results in overflow an exception should be generated. The following figure may help you to organize your thoughts in solving this exercise.

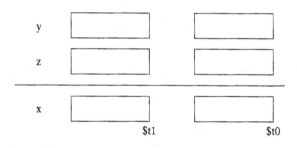

After writing your code, calculate the following performance indexes:

Space: _____(Words of code)

Time: _____(Maximum number of clock cycles to execute)

9.14 When the MIPS `mult` instruction is executed, a 64-bit product is produced. Many programs doing numerical calculations are designed to process only 32-bit results. For applications written to perform 32-bit precision arithmetic, it is extremely important to detect when the product of two numbers cannot be represented with 32 bits, so that some alternative function may be invoked. Write a reentrant library function anyone could use called *MUL32 (m, n, p)*. All function parameters will be passed on the stack. If the product of the two input arguments *m* and *n* cannot be represented with 32 bits (assuming the two's complement number system), then an exception should be generated.

Provide in-line comments and write a paragraph in English to describe all of the conditions that your code tests for to detect overflow. (*Hint:* The XOR instruction can be useful when writing this function.)

With this function, you will demonstrate how to write MIPS assembly language code involving nested function calls. Write a function to perform a vector product. *vectorprod (&X, &Y, &Z, N, status)*. Vectorprod will call the *MUL32* function. Use the stack to pass arguments. The in parameters are the starting address of three different word arrays (vectors)—X, Y, Z—and an integer value N specifying the size of the vectors. Status is an out parameter to indicate if overflow ever occurred while executing this function. The function will perform the vector product

$$X_i = Y_i * Z_i, \text{ with i going from 0 to N} - 1$$

Write a MIPS assembly language *main* program that could be used to test the *vectorprod* function.

CHAPTER 10

A Pipelined Implementation

There are 10 kinds of people in this world:
Those who know binary and those who don't.

10.1 INTRODUCTION

In the previous chapters of this textbook, we developed assembly language code for a simplified model of the MIPS architecture. To build a processor that will run almost five times faster than the simplified model a technique called **pipelining** is used in all actual implementations of the MIPS architecture. Essentially, this speedup is accomplished by utilizing a concept analogous to Henry Ford's method of building cars on an assembly line. In accordance with this concept, the CPU chip is designed to process each instruction by passing information through a series of functional units. In a five-stage pipeline implementation, there are five different stages of hardware within the processor to process an instruction. With a five-stage pipelined implementation, we will have five different instructions at different stages of execution moving through the pipeline. It takes five clock cycles for any instruction to work its way through the pipeline, but since there are five instructions being executed simultaneously, the average execution rate is one instruction per clock cycle. The functions performed in these five stages are as follows:

1. **Instruction Fetch Stage.** Fetch the instruction from cache memory and load it into the instruction register. Increment the program counter by four.
2. **Operand Fetch Stage.** Fetch values Rs and Rt from the register file. If this is a branch instruction and the branch condition is met, then load the PC with the branch target address.
3. **Execute Stage.** Perform an arithmetic or logic function in the ALU and load the result register. This is the stage where an addition is performed to calculate the effective address for a load or store instruction.

4. **Memory Access Stage.** If the instruction is a load, a read from the data cache occurs. If the instruction is a store, write to the data to cache occurs. Otherwise, pass the data in the result register on to the write back register.

5. **Write Back Stage.** Store the value in the write back register to the register file. Notice that when the first instruction into the pipeline is storing results back to the register file, the fourth instruction into the pipeline is simultaneously reading from the register file.

10.2   A PIPELINED DATAPATH

Figure 10.1 shows a five-stage datapath diagram with all the major components identified. It is important to understand that during each clock cycle all five pipeline stages are performing their function and passing their results on to the next pipeline stage via pipeline registers. The IR is the pipeline register that holds the results of the **instruction fetch** stage. Registers Rs and Rt hold the results of the **operand fetch** stage. The result register holds the result of the **execute** stage. In the **data access** stage, the write back register holds the data read from memory in the case of a load instruction, and for all other instructions it is a pipeline register holding the value that was in the result register at the end of the previous clock cycle. The **write back** stage is simple. During the first half of the fifth clock period, the information in the write back register is stored into the register file. Accomplishing a write back to the register file in the first half of the clock cycle will then allow any instruction that is at the second stage of the pipeline to read out this new value during the second half of the same clock cycle. A pipelined processor creates new challenges for the assembly language programmer. Specifically, these challenges are the result of data hazards and control hazards.

10.3   DATA HAZARD

The term **data hazard** refers to the following situation. Suppose we have three sequential instructions x, y, and z that come into the pipeline, and suppose also that x is the first instruction into the pipeline followed by y and z. If the results computed by instruction x are needed by y or z, then we have a data hazard. The hardware solution to this problem is to include **forwarding** paths in the machine's datapath so that even though the results have not yet been written back to the register file, the needed information is forwarded from the result register or the write back register to the input of the ALU.

One type of data hazard cannot be solved with forwarding hardware. This is a situation where a load instruction (`lw` or `lb`) is immediately followed by an instruction that would use the value fetched from memory. The only solution to this problem is to rearrange the assembly language code so that the instruction following the load is not an instruction that uses the value being fetched from memory. In recognition of this situation we refer to load instructions on pipelined processors as being **delayed loads**. If the existing instructions in the algorithm cannot be rearranged to solve the data hazard then a **no-operation** (nop) instruction is placed in memory immediately following the load instruction. We are assured that the state of the machine is not affected by the execution of the nop as it passes through the pipeline, but it does provide enough time delay so

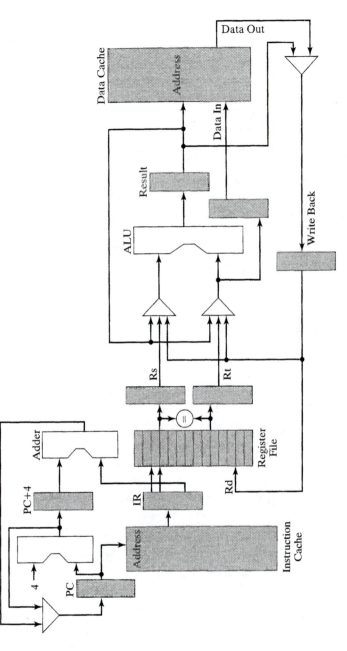

FIGURE 10.1

Pipelined Datapath Diagram

that the next instruction in sequence will have access to a valid copy of the value read from memory by the preceeding load instruction.

The assembler translates the nop mnemonic to 0x00000000 in binary, which is also the binary code for the instruction sll $0 $0 0.

10.4   CONTROL HAZARD

Associated with *every* branch or jump instruction we have a **control hazard**. Referring to section 10.1 and the functions performed at each stage of the pipeline, we see that during the first clock cycle of any branch or jump instruction the instruction is fetched. During the second clock cycle, two values are read from the register file as specified by the Rs and Rt fields of the branch instruction, and during this same clock cycle these two operand values are compared to determine whether they are equal or not. If the branch condition is met, then the sign-extended immediate field within the branch instruction is added to the PC. While all this is going on, the instruction following the branch or jump is being fetched. So if the branch condition is met, then during the third clock cycle the instruction at the newly computed target address in the PC will be used to fetch the next instruction. But while this third instruction is being fetched, the instruction that immediately followed the branch or jump will be in the second stage of the pipeline. Since the branch cannot take effect until the second stage of the pipeline, we say that it is a **delayed branch**. Essentially, there is no way to eliminate the control hazards, so the solution is to recognize that a branch or jump instruction will take effect after the instruction following the branch or jump is in the pipeline. This means that a programmer must recognize this fact and organize the code to take this into account. Typically, a programmer will find some MIPS instruction in the code that the branch is not dependent on that preceded the branch and will place it in the **delay slot** following the branch. If the existing instructions in the algorithm cannot be rearranged to solve the control hazard, then a nop instruction is placed in memory immediately following the branch instruction.

Most commercial MIPS assemblers detect hazards in the source assembly language code. These assemblers will attempt to rearrange the code if possible, and if not, they will automatically insert nop instructions to eliminate the hazards. The PCSpim assembler does not provide this feature, so it is your responsibility to eliminate data hazards and control hazards when running PCSpim in its pipelined mode.

10.5   PCSPIM OPTION TO SIMULATE A PIPELINED IMPLEMENTATION

PCSpim provides an option to run the simulator as if it were a pipelined implementation of the MIPS architecture. To invoke this option, go to **Settings** under the simulation pull-down menu and click the **Delayed Branches** and **Delayed Load** boxes. Using this option, you will gain experience in writing assembly language code that will run on a pipelined implementation of the MIPS architecture. Here again, we see the advantages of using the PCSpim simulator to become familiar with these important concepts. When you single step through a program, you will see that every instruction following a branch or jump is always executed. The system calls are not delayed, so leave those portions of your code unchanged.

10.6   SUM OF INTEGERS RUNNING IN PIPELINED MODE

The first example program presented in this textbook (Section 2.11) is repeated here. This program is used to find the sum of the integers from 1 to N, where N is a value entered from the keyboard. If you attempt to run this program with PCSpim in pipelined mode, you will find that it ends up in an infinite loop. Look at the four instructions starting at the label "Loop." You will notice that the instruction following the branch instruction

```
        .data
prompt: .asciiz\"n Please input a value for N = "
result: .asciiz\" The sum of the integers from 1 to N is"
bye:    .asciiz \"n **** Adios Amigo - Have a good day *****
        .globl main
        .text                       text # For a Pipelined Implementation
main:                       main:
        li      $v0,4       #        li      $v0, 4          #
        la      $a0, prompt #        la      $a0, prompt
        syscall             #        syscall

        li      $v0, 5      #        li      $v0, 5          #
        syscall             #        syscall                #
        blez    $v0, End    #        blez    $v0, End        #
        li      $t0, 0      #        move    $t0, $v0        #***
Loop:                       Loop:
        add     $t0, $t0, $v0 #      addi    $v0, $v0, -1    #
        addi    $v0, $v0,-1 #        bnez    $v0, Loop       #
        bnez    $v0, Loop   #        add     $t0, $t0, $v0   #***

        li      $v0, 4      #        li      $v0, 4          #
        la      $a0, result #        la      $a0, result     #
        syscall             #        syscall                #
        li      $v0,1       #        li      $v0, 1          #
        move    $a0, $t0    #        move    $a0, $t0        #
        syscall             #        syscall                #
        b       main        #        b       main           #
End:    li      $v0, 4      #   End: li      $v0, 4          #
        la      $a0, bye    #        la      $a0, bye        #
        syscall             #        syscall                #

        li      $v0, 10     #        li      $v0, 10         #
        syscall             #        syscall                #
```

loads $v0 with the value 4. When PCSpim is in pipelined mode, this instruction will always get executed because it is in the **delay slot**. Thus, $v0 never becomes zero, so the program loops until overflow occurs. Here is the code:

You will notice that only two instructions had to be changed to make this program function correctly in pipelined mode. If possible, we always place a useful instruction in the delay slot. Since the branch is dependent on the results created by decrementing $v0, we cannot place this instruction in the delay slot. With a little thought, we realize that if we initialize $t0 with the initial value of N, then we can place the instruction that is accumulating the sum in the delay slot.

10.7   A FUNCTION CALL IN PIPELINED MODE

The next figure shows how the example program that finds the sum of the positive values and the sum of the negative values (Section 5.4) must be modified to run on a pipelined implementation of the MIPS architecture. Only one change was made to the main program. One of the arguments passed to the Sum function is the size of the array, which in this example is four. You will notice the `li $a1, 4` instruction has been placed in the **delay slot** after the `jal Sum`. Have no fear: The load immediate instruction is in the pipeline before any of the instructions associated with the Sum function, so this size parameter has indeed been passed to the function.

Within the Sum function, a number of modifications are required. We begin by looking for instructions to place in the delay slots. Swapping the two instructions at the label "Negative" is a good start. We can also move the instruction `add $v0, $v0, $t0` that immediately precedes the `b Loop` into its delay slot. This last modification leaves two branch instructions back-to-back, which is a definite problem. We have to find some instruction to place in the delay slot after the `bltz $t0, Negative` instruction. There is only one acceptable candidate: `addi $a1, $a1, -1`. Do you see why? We have to place some instruction in the slot following the `lw $t0, 0($a0)` because of the data hazard, and the instruction `addi $a0, $a0, 4` is the only instruction we can place in this slot. Finally, you will notice that a `nop` was placed after the `jr $ra` instruction because the next location in memory could contain any instruction, and we certainly don't want this program executing some random instruction every time it perform a return to the main program. The code is on page 95.

10.8 AN EXAMPLE WHERE NOPS CANNOT BE AVOIDED

In some situations, there is no way to avoid using a few nops. In this final example, you will notice that three nops have been placed in the modified code. Does this mean that the modified code will take longer to execute? The answer is no, because for a pipelined machine the average execution speed is nearly five times faster than an equivalent machine that is not pipelined. The additional nops going through the pipeline are there only to provide some delay. They perform no useful work, so every additional nop that is introduced will have some effect on the execution rate of a pipelined machine, but usually the effect is quite small. The effective execution rate will only be slightly less than five times faster than an equivalent machine that is not pipelined.

The MinMax function presented next is designed to search through an array of 32-bit words and to return the minimum and maximum values found in the array. A number of modifications are necessary for this function to execute in pipelined mode. The first thing we need to do is to find some instruction to place in the delay slot at the end of the first five instructions. After careful analysis, we find the instruction : `move $v1, $v0` is probably the best candidate to be placed in the delay slot. Notice that this instruction uses the value being read from memory. It would be a mistake to move the `addiu $a0, $a0, 4` instruction into the delay slot because we would end up with : `move $v1, $v0` immediately after the load instruction, and this is not good because the data being read from memory that's going to $v0 will not be available for one more clock cycle.

There are five instructions in the next block of code starting with the label "Loop." There are two branch instructions in this block of code, so we need to find instructions to place in the delay slot of each branch instruction. We have to leave some instruction that is not dependent on the value being read from memory in the delay slot of the load.

```
        .data
array: .word    -4, 5, 8, -1
msg1:  .asciiz "\n The sum of the positive values = "
msg2:  .asciiz "\n The sum of the negative values = "
       .globl main
       .text
main:
       li      $v0, 4      # system ca
       la      $a0, msg1   # load addr
       syscall             # print the
       la      $a0, array  # Initializ
       li      $a1, 4      # Initializ
       jal     Sum         # Call sum
       move    $a0, $v0    # move valu
       li      $v0, 1      # system cl
       syscall             # print sum
       li      $v0, 4      # system ca
       la      $a0, msg2   # load addr
       syscall             # print the
       li      $v0, 1      # system ca
       move    $a0, $v1    # move valu
       syscall             # print sum
       li      $v0, 10     #
       syscall             #
############################
# $a0: Pointer to Array
# $a1: Number of elements
############################
Sum:   li      $v0, 0
       li      $v1, 0
Loop:
       blez    $a1, Return   # If(a1 <=0
       addi    $a1, $a1, -1  # Decrement
       lw      $t0, 0($a0)   # Get a val
       addi    $a0, $a0, 4   # Increment
       bltz    $t0, Negative # If value
       add     $v0, $v0, $t0 # Add to po
       b       Loop          # Branch ar
Negative:
       add     $v1, $v1, $t0 # Add to th
       b       Loop          # Branch to
Return:
       jr      $ra           # Return
```

```
           .globl main
           .text # Modified for Pipeline Run
main:
           li      $v0, 4       #
           la      $a0, msg1    #
           syscall              #
           la      $a0, array   #
           jal     Sum          #
           li      $a1, 4       #***
           move    $a0, $v0     #
           li      $v0, 1       #
           syscall              #
           li      $v0, 4       #
           la      $a0, msg2    #
           syscall              #
           li      $v0, 1       #
           move    $a0,$v1      #
           syscall              #
           li      $v0, 10      #
           syscall              #
#########################################
#$a0: Pointer to Array                  #
#$a1: Number of elements                #
#########################################
Sum:       li      $v0, 0
           li      $v1, 0
Loop:
           blez    $a1, Return   #
           lw      $t0, 0($a0)   #
           addi    $a0, $a0, 4   #
           bltz    $t0, Negative #
           addi    $a1, $a1, -1  #***
           b       Loop          #
           add     $v0, $v0, $t0 #***
Negative:
           b       Loop          #
           add     $v1, $v1, $t0 #***
Return:
           jr      $ra           #
           nop                   #***
```

We are left with the unavoidable necessity of placing a nop after the first branch instruction and swapping the order of the last two instructions in this block.

Near the end of the code, at the label chk, we find two instructions. The first instruction decrements a loop counter, and the second instruction tests the decremented value. Thus, it appears that we will have to place a nop in the delay slot of this branch instruction. With more careful analysis, you may actually find a way to eliminate this nop.

Compilers translate high-level code to assembly language code. The final phase of this translation is called code generation. Whoever writes the program to do code generation has to be aware of the special requirements associated with a pipelined implementation.

Following is the code for the MinMax function:

```
##########################################
# MinMax ($a0: Address, $a1: Number word
#         $v0: Minimum, $v1: Maximum)
##########################################
        .global MinMax
        .text                          .text # Pipelined Implementation
MinMax:                        MinMax:
        lw      $v0, 0($a0)            lw      $v0, 0($a0)     #
        addiu   $a0, $a0,4            addiu   $a0, $a0,4       #
        move    $v1, $v0             addi    $a1, $a1,-1       #
        addi    $a1, $a1,-1          blez    $a1, ret         #
        blez    $a1, ret             move    $v1, $v0         #***
loop:                          loop:
        lw      $t0, 0($a0)           lw      $t0, 0($a0)     #
        addi    $a0, $a0,4           addi    $a0, $a0,4        #
        bge     $t0, $v0,next        bge     $t0, $v0,next    #
        move    $v0, $t0             nop                      #***
        b       chk                  b       chk              #
next:                                move    $v0, $t0         #***
        ble     $t0, $v1,chk  next:
        move    $v1, $t0             ble     $t0, $v1,chk     #
chk:                                 move    $v1, $t0         #
        addi    $a1, $a1, -1  chk:
        bnez    $a1,loop             addi    $a1, $a1, -1     #
ret:                                 bnez    $a1,loop         #
        jr      $ra                  nop                      #***
                               ret:
                                     jr      $ra              #
                                     nop                      #***
```

EXERCISES

In the following exercises, run the PCSpim simulator in the mode where it simulates a pipelined implementation of the MIPS architecture. If you cannot eliminate the hazards in your code by rearranging the code, then insert nop instructions to eliminate the hazards.

10.1 Write a MIPS function to search through an array X of N words to find how many of the values in the array are evenly divisible by four. The address of the array will be passed to the function using register $a0, and the number of words in the array will be passed in register $a1. Return your results in register $v0.

10.2 Write a MIPS function to sort an array X of N words into ascending order using the bubble sort algorithm. The address of the array and the value N will be passed to the function on the stack.

10.3 Write a MIPS function, *Adduovf* (x, y, s), that will find the 32-bit sum s of two unsigned arguments x and y. An exception should be generated if the unsigned representation of the sum results in overflow.

10.4 Write a MIPS function to return the Nth element in the Fibonacci sequence. A value N is passed to the function on the stack, and the Nth Fibonacci number E is returned on the stack. If N is greater than 46, overflow will occur, so return a value of 0 if N is greater than 46. Also, show an example of calling this function to return the tenth element in the sequence. The first few numbers in the Fibonacci sequence are 0, 1, 1, 2, 3, 5, ...

CHAPTER 11

Floating-Point Instructions

What did the hot dog say when he crossed the finish line?
I'm the wiener!

11.1   INTRODUCTION

Typically **floating-point numbers** are used in scientific and engineering calculations. For example the velocity of light is 186,281.7 miles per second. A light year, the distance traveled by light in one year is 5,880,000,000,000 miles. The atomic weight of hydrogen is 1.008. A micron, which is one millionth of a meter, is 0.00000003937 inch. Each of these numbers is represented in *normalized* scientific notation as follows:

$$0.1862817 \times 10^{+6}$$
$$0.588 \times 10^{+13}$$
$$0.1008 \times 10^{1}$$
$$0.3937 \times 10^{-7}$$

How can we encode this huge **range** of numbers in binary? In 1985, the Institute of Electrical and Electronics Engineers (IEEE) established a standard for representing floating-point numbers and also established some standards regarding how floating-point calculations would be performed to insure a certain degree of accuracy (IEEE 754). A 32-bit (single-precision), and a 64-bit (double-precision) standard have also been established. In the single-precision format, 7 decimal digits of precision can be encoded, and the exponent scale factor has a range of approximately 10^{+-38}. In the double-precision format, 16 decimal digits of precision can be encoded, and the exponent scale factor has a range of approximately 10^{+-308}.

Appendix F provides a list of floating-point instructions for the MIPS architecture. Within the MIPS architectural description, the floating-point hardware unit is referred to as **Coprocessor 1**. Coprocessor 1 has its own hardware to perform floating-point arithmetic. Notice that in Appendix F there are both single-precision and double-precision instructions to perform addition, subtraction, multiplication, and division. There are instructions to perform the absolute value, to negate, and to move a copy of a value in a source floating-point register to a destination floating-point register. There are six different instructions to compare the contents of two floating-point registers. If the comparison condition is met, then a special status flag associated with Coprocessor 1 is set. There are two branch instructions specifically designed to test this status flag, bc1t (Branch if flag is true) and bc1f (Branch if flag is false). Other instructions to move values between the general-purpose register file and the floating-point register file, as well as instructions to perform number conversions from one type to another, are also found in Appendix F.

11.2 THE FLOATING-POINT REGISTER FILE

Coprocessor 1 has a register file that can be visualized as sixteen 64-bit registers or as thirty-two 32-bit registers. The operands for all the floating-point instructions are accessed from the floating-point register file. Double-precision instructions operate on a pair of these adjacent 32-bit registers. All double-precision floating-point instructions require the source and destination registers be specified as even-numbered registers. For example mul.s $f0, $f12, $f14

The following is the established register usage convention for the floating-point registers:

$f0 - $f3	Function-returned values
$f4 - $f11	Temporary values
$f12 - $f15	Arguments passed into a function
$f16 - $f19	More temporary values
$f20 - $f31	Saved values

Notice the system services to read values from the keyboard and to print values to the monitor follow this convention. When you read a floating-point number, the system service returns the value in register $f0. To print a floating-point number, pass the value to the system service in register $f12.

11.3 EXAMPLES

Suppose we want to accurately compute the area of a circle with a radius of 12.345678901234567 inches and print the result as a double-precision floating-point number. (Area = $\pi * r^2$) The following MIPS program will accomplish the task:

```
        .data
Pi:     .double      3.1415926535897924
Rad:    .double      12.345678901234567
        .text
main:   l.d     $f0, Pi        # $f0 = Pi
        l.d     $f4, Rad       # $f4 = Radius
        mul.d   $f12, $f4, $f4   # $f12 = Radius squared
        mul.d   $f12, $f12, $f0  # Multiply by Pi
```

```
        li      $v0, 3          #
        syscall                 # Print the area
        li      $v0, 10         #
        syscall                 # Terminate run
```

(This would be a good time to refer to the assembler directives in Appendix A, where you will find a description of the .double and .float assembler directives.)

The next example provides a demonstration of the **compare less than or equal** c.le.s instruction and the **branch if floating-point condition flag is true** bc1t instruction. When a compare instruction is executed two floating-point registers are compared. If the specified condition is met, then a condition flag in Coprocessor 1 is set to one (true), else the condition flag is cleared to zero (false). When this program runs, you may be surprised to see that the decimal value 12.2 cannot be represented exactly in binary. You will learn why later in this chapter. Here is the code:

```
################################################################
#  Functional Description:
#  Start with a binary value in $f13 approximately equal to the
#  decimal value 12.2.
#  Decrement $f13 by one each iteration until the value in $f13 is
#  less than 1.0
################################################################
        .data
Num:    .float  12.2
one:    .float  1.0
cr:     .asciiz "\n"
        .text
main:
        l.s     $f13, Num       # Load $f13 with the 12.2
        l.s     $f1, one        # Load $f1 with the value 1.0
        la      $a0, cr         # $a0 gets address of cr
loop:
        li      $v0, 2          # Print single precision result
        mov.s   $f12, $f13
        syscall

        sub.s   $f13, $f13, $f1  # Subtract 1.0 from $f13
        c.le.s  $f1, $f13        # If ($f1 <= $f13) set cond. flag
                                 # Else clear condition flag in CP1

        li      $v0, 4
        syscall                  # Newline
        bc1t    loop             # Branch if condition flag is true
        li      $v0, 10          # Terminate run
        syscall
################################################################
```

The first three instructions in the preceding program are macro instructions. If you analyze the code generated by the assembler you will see that these three macro instructions expand into six real instructions. A knowledgeable MIPS assembly language programmer interested in writing optimized code would replace the first three macro instructions in this program, which the assembler expands into six real instructions with the following four instructions:

```
la      $a3, Base       # $a3 points to data segment
lwc1    $f13, 0($a3)    # Load $f13 with the 12.2
lwc1    $f1, 4($a3)     # Load $f1 with the value 1.0
addiu   $a0, $a3, 8     # $a0 gets address of cr
```

In the optimized code, register $a3 is loaded with the base address of the data segment. The first word in the data segment, with an offset of zero, contains a single-precision floating-point binary value that is close to the decimal value 12.2. The second word in the data segment, with an offset of four, contains the value 1.0 encoded in single-precision IEEE 754 floating-point representation. The address of the ASCII code for carriage return is the base address of the data segment plus eight. Notice that in the optimized code we are using the instruction *load word Coprocessor 1*, whose mnemonic is lwc1.

11.4 BINARY FLOATING-POINT TO DECIMAL FLOATING-POINT CONVERSION

In general, a floating-point number has an integer part and a fractional part. For example, given the floating-point decimal number 295.48, 295 is the integer part and 0.48 is the fractional part. Any decimal floating-point number has a polynomial expansion. For example, the polynomial expansion for the decimal value 295.48 is

$$2 * 10^2 + 9 * 10^1 + 5 * 10^0 + 4 * 10^{-1} + 8 * 10^{-2}$$

By the same token, a binary floating-point number has a polynomial expansion. For example, the polynomial expansion for the binary floating-point value 101.101_2 is

$$1 * 2^2 + 0 * 2^1 + 1 * 2^0 + 1 * 2^{-1} + 0 * 2^{-2} + 1 * 2^{-3}$$

Finding the decimal equivalent of any floating-point binary number simply involves evaluating the polynomial expansion. The following table of the powers of two is extremely useful in performing this conversion process:

2^4	2^3	2^2	2^1	2^0	2^{-1}	2^{-2}	2^{-3}	2^{-4}	2^{-5}	2^{-6}
16	8	4	2	1	0.5	0.25	0.125	0.0625	0.03125	0.015625

Using this table, we evaluate the polynomial for the binary number 101.101_2 as

$$1 * 4 + 0 * 2 + 1 * 1 + 1 * 0.5 + 0 * 0.25 + 1 * 0.125 = 5.625$$

Therefore, the binary number 101.101 is equivalent to 5.625 in the decimal number system. You will notice that to expand the table for the powers of two to the left, you simply multiply the previous value by 2, and to expand the table to the right, you divide the previous value by 2.

11.5   DECIMAL FLOATING-POINT TO BINARY FLOATING-POINT CONVERSION

Converting a decimal floating-point number to its equivalent binary floating-point representation involves two different processes. As a result of what you learned in Chapter 3, you already know how to convert a decimal integer number to its equivalent binary representation. Recall that the process involves repeatedly dividing by 2 and recording the remainder after each division. For example, the decimal value 25 is equivalent to 11001 in binary. Suppose we want to find the binary floating-point equivalent of the decimal number 25.25.

The process of finding the binary equivalent of the decimal fraction portion involves repeatedly multiplying the decimal fraction by 2 and recording the integer value portion of 1 or 0 that is produced. In other words, we record the resulting integer that is produced by doubling the decimal fraction. This first integer produced will be the first digit after the binary point. As you know from the previous section, the value 0.1 in binary corresponds to one-half (0.5) in the decimal number system. So obviously if we start with a decimal fraction of one-half or greater and we double this fractional value we will get an integer 1 produced, which will be the first binary digit to the right of the binary point in the binary equivalent. Upon recording the integer portion that is produced, we focus our attention on the resulting fractional portion of the previously doubled value. We repeatedly perform the doubling process on the fractional portions. Each integer value produced is the next binary digit to the right of the previous. We stop the process when we end up with zero for a fractional result. For some decimal numbers this process will never end because we will never get zero in the fractional portion. This is analogous to the fact that the decimal value one-third cannot be expressed exactly as a decimal number. But as you know the decimal value 0.333333333333333333333333333 is a close approximation. Given this procedure, let's find the binary equivalent of the decimal value 0.25:

	0.25
First digit after binary point	0.5
Second digit after binary point	1.0
Done	

So we now can say that the decimal value 25.25 is represented in binary as 11001.01. As a second example, we will convert the decimal vale 12.2 to binary. We should have no difficulty in finding that the decimal value 12 is represented in binary as 1100. We now need to find the binary equivalent of the decimal fraction 0.2:

	0.2
First digit after binary point	0.4
Second digit after binary point	0.8
Third digit after binary point	1.6
Forth digit after binary point	1.2
The above sequence repeats forever.	

So we now can say that the decimal value 12.2 cannot be represented exactly in binary, but a close approximation is 1100.00110011001100110011001100110011001100110011. An abbreviated representation for this repeating fractional portion is indicated by drawing a line above the repeating pattern:

$$1100.\overline{0011}$$

11.6   THE IEEE 754 FLOATING-POINT STANDARD

The IEEE 754 single-precision floating-point format is as follows:

1-bit	8-bit	23-bit
Sign	Biased exponent	Significand

The IEEE 754 single precision floating-point format specifies three distinct fields:

- The sign of the number (0: positive, 1: negative)
- The biased exponent (The actual exponent value plus 127)
- A value for the significand, which is the magnitude of the fractional portion

Negative numbers are not expressed in the two's complement representation with this standard. Numbers are expressed in a sign-magnitude representation. The value in the exponent field does not have an explicit sign. The unsigned binary value in the exponent field is 127 greater than the actual exponent for the number. As an example, if we find the value 130 in the biased exponent field, then we know that the actual exponent is three. To explain what gets stored in the significand field, an example is presented. Recall that 11001.01 is the binary equivalent of 25.25 in the decimal number system. Use the following procedure to encode a binary floating-point value in the IEEE format:

- Enter a value for the sign bit (0: positive, 1: negative).
- Normalize the binary representation so that the binary point is to the right of the first 1. Determine the exponent value. If we move the binary point to the left when normalizing, we will have a positive exponent corresponding to the number of digit positions the binary point was moved. If we move the binary point to the right, we will have a negative exponent corresponding to the number of digit positions the binary point was moved. For the decimal value 25.25, the normalized binary representation is

$$1.100001 \times 2^4$$

- Add 127 (01111111) to the *actual* exponent, and place this value into the 8-bit biased exponent field. For this example, we would get

$$127 + 4 = \underset{10}{131} = (\underset{2}{10000011})$$

- Fill in the 23-bit significand field with all the digits to the right of the binary point that appear in the normalized representation. Now you may ask, "What about the 1 to the left of the binary point?" This bit is *not* stored anywhere. Since all normalized numbers (except zero) have a leading 1, this bit does not occupy a position within the encoding. This implicit bit is called the **hidden bit**.

Here is the value 12.25 encoded in the IEEE Format:

0	1 0 0 0 0 0 1 1	1 0 0 0 0 1 0 0 0 0 0 0 0 0 0 0 0 0 0 0 0 0 0

The hardware that performs floating-point arithmetic always recreates the hidden bit when floating-point values are manipulated by the hardware. A programmer writing I/O algorithms to convert values between their floating-point binary representation and their ASCII decimal representation must be cognizant of the requirement to re-create the hidden bit.

The floating-point value zero (0.0) has a special encoding, as well as a set of values referred to as denormalized numbers, in which case the hidden bit is "re-created" as a *zero*. The value zero in the **biased exponent** field indicates a denormalized interpretation for a set of extremely small values. There are other special codes to represent positive infinity, negative infinity, and something called **Not a Number** (NaN). The value 255 (all ones) in the biased exponent field indicates that this special interpretation must be used. Hardware produces the code for NaN when illegal operations are performed such as infinity divided by infinity, or the square root of a negative number. The MIPS floating-point unit (Coprocessor 1) generates an exception whenever **overflow**, **underflow**, or division by zero occurs. When any finite number is divided by zero, the code for infinity is stored in the destination register. Infinity plus anything results in infinity. Any finite number divided by infinity produces zero. The following table provides a convenient reference to interpret these special IEEE 754 encodings.

Interpretation	Sign	Exponent	Significand
Zero	0/1	00000000	00000000000000000000000
Denormalized	0/1	00000000	Any nonzero value
Infinity	0/1	11111111	00000000000000000000000
Not a Number	0/1	11111111	Any nonzero value

It is interesting to note that, given two positive floating-point numbers encoded in IEEE 754 representation, it is possible to make a comparison for greater than or less than using the same hardware used to do an unsigned binary–integer comparison. This no doubt is the major reason the IEEE standard specifies a biased exponent.

11.7 DECODING NUMBERS: THE IEEE 754 FLOATING-POINT STANDARD

The rules for decoding a binary floating-point number will now be developed. A specific example will be provided to demonstrate the rules. Suppose we are given the following IEEE single-precision binary floating-point representation for a number, and we want to determine the equivalent value as a floating-point decimal number:

| 1 | 1 0 0 0 0 1 0 1 | 0 0 1 1 0 1 1 0 0 0 0 0 0 0 0 0 0 0 0 0 0 0 0 |

- The first bit indicates the sign of the number (0: positive, 1: negative). For this example, we have a negative decimal number encoded.
- Subtract 127 from the value found in the biased exponent field to determine the actual exponent. For this example the actual exponent is 6. ($133 - 127 = 6$)
- Using the significand bits write the number in normalized binary representation. Remember to include the recreated hidden bit and an indication of the sign of the number. For this example, we have -1.0011011×2^6
- Denormalize the number by moving the binary point the number of positions indicated by the actual exponent. For our example, the denormalized number is

$$-1001101.1$$

- In the final step, we simply perform a binary-to-decimal conversion by evaluating the polynomial expansion of the binary number. For this example, we determine that -77.5 is the equivalent decimal value.

The IEEE 754 double-precision floating-point format follows the same rules as the single-precision format except that 64-bits are used to encode a number as follows:

- The sign of the number (0: positive, 1: negative)
- An 11-bit biased exponent (the actual exponent value plus 1023)
- A 52-bit significand, which is the magnitude of the fractional portion

11.8 A SMALL 8-BIT FLOATING-POINT FORMAT

Often it is difficult to appreciate some of the subtleties of the IEEE 754 floating-point format because we are dealing with such a large range of values. A small 8-bit floating-point format is presented in this section, as a pedagogical aid to understanding some of these subtleties.

Any floating-point representation involves a trade-off between range and precision. With 8 bits, we have 256 unique binary patterns. This small 8-bit floating-point format has all the characteristics of the IEEE standard, except that it involves fewer bits. This small pedagogical 8-bit floating-point format is defined as follows, with the decimal value **-6.75** encoded:

```
1-bit  3-bit Biased  4-bit
Sign   Exponent      Significand
```

| 1 | 1 0 1 | 1 0 1 1 |

This small format specifies three distinct fields:

- The sign of the number (0: positive, 1: negative)
- The biased exponent (the actual exponent value plus 3)
- A value for the significand, which is the magnitude of the fractional portion

Here we demonstrate the steps involved in decoding the example value shown in this small floating-point format:

- The first bit indicates the sign of the number. (0: positive, 1: negative) For this example, we have a negative decimal number encoded.
- Subtract three from the value found in the biased exponent field to determine the actual exponent. For this example, the actual exponent is two. $(5 - 3 = 2)$
- Using the significand bits write the number in normalized binary representation. Remember to include the recreated hidden bit and an indication of the sign of the number. For this example, we have -1.1011×2^2.
- Denormalize the number by moving the binary point the number of positions indicated by the actual exponent. For our example, the denormalized number is

$$-110.11$$

- In the final step we simply perform a binary to decimal conversion by evaluating the polynomial expansion of the binary number. For this example, we determine that -6.75 is the equivalent decimal value.

Table 11.1 shows the range of numbers that can be encoded using this small floating-point format. This table shows some interesting representative values. A complete table would have 256 entries. Following are the four different interpretations applied in this table:

- D—Denormalized
- N—Normalized
- Inf—Infinity
- NaN—Not a Number

The column furthest to the right indicates the *gap* between adjacent values using this encoding. You will notice for the larger values the gap is 0.5, whereas for the smaller values the gap is 0.0078125. The gap at any particular location in the table is a function of the actual exponent e and the number of bits of precision in the significand. The generalized formula for computing the gap for any floating-point representation is $2^{(e\text{-precision})}$.

With the small floating-point format we have 4-bits of **precision**, and for the larger numbers in this format the exponent "e" is 3; thus, the gap is $2^{(3-4)} = 2^{-1} = 0.5$. For the smaller values, the exponent is -3; thus, the gap is $2^{-7} = 0.0078125$. For the IEEE 32-bit, single-precision floating-point format, we have 23 bits of precision, and for the larger numbers in this format, the exponent e is 128. From this information, we can compute the gap between the larger values encoded in the IEEE 32-bit single-precision floating-point format as $2^{(128-23)} = 2^{105}$ and the gap between the smaller values as 2^{-150}.

TABLE 11.1   Representative values encoded in the small floating-point format

Sign	Biased Exponent	Significant	Interpretation	Magnitude Binary	Magnitude Decimal	Gap
0/1	000	0000	D	0.000	Zero	
0/1	000	0001	D	0.0001×2^{-3}	0.0078125 = 1/128	0.0078125
0/1	000	0010	D	0.0010×2^{-3}	0.015625 = 1/64	0.0078125
0/1	000	0011	D	0.0011×2^{-3}	0.0234375 = 3/128	0.0078125
0/1	000	0100	D	0.0100×2^{-3}	0.03125 = 1/32	0.0078125
—	—	—	—	—	—	—
0/1	000	1000	D	0.1000×2^{-3}	0.0625 = 1/16	0.0078125
—	—	—	—	—	—	—
0/1	000	1111	D	0.1111×2^{-3}	0.1171875 = 15/128	0.0078125
0/1	001	0000	N	1.0000×2^{-2}	0.25 = 1/4	0.1328125
—	—	—	—	—	—	—
0/1	001	1111	N	1.1111×2^{-2}	0.484375 = 31/64	0.015625
0/1	010	0000	N	1.0000×2^{-1}	0.5 = ½	0.015625
0/1	010	0001	N	1.0001×2^{-1}	0.503125 = 17/32	0.03125
—	—	—	—	—	—	—
0/1	010	1111	N	1.1111×2^{-1}	0.96875 = 31/32	0.03125
0/1	011	0000	N	1.0000	1.0	0.03125
0/1	011	0001	N	1.0001	1.0625	0.0625
—	—	—	—	—	—	—
0/1	011	1111	N	1.1111	1.96875	0.0625
0/1	100	0000	N	$1.0000 \times 2^{+1}$	2.0	0.0625
0/1	100	0001	N	$1.0001 \times 2^{+1}$	2.125	0.125
—	—	—	—	—	—	—
0/1	100	1111	N	$1.1111 \times 2^{+1}$	3.875	0.125
0/1	101	0000	N	$1.0000 \times 2^{+2}$	4.0	0.125
0/1	101	0001	N	$1.0001 \times 2^{+2}$	4.25	0.25
—	—	—	—	—	—	—
0/1	101	1111	N	$1.1111 \times 2^{+2}$	7.75	0.25
0/1	110	0000	N	$1.0000 \times 2^{+3}$	8.0	0.25
0/1	110	0001	N	$1.0001 \times 2^{+3}$	8.5	0.5
—	—	—	—	—	—	—
0/1	110	1100	N	$1.1100 \times 2^{+3}$	14.0	0.5
0/1	110	1101	N	$1.1101 \times 2^{+3}$	14.5	0.5
0/1	110	1110	N	$1.1110 \times 2^{+3}$	15.0	0.5
0/1	110	1111	N	$1.1111 \times 2^{+3}$	15.5	0.5
0	111	0000	+Inf	Positive Infinity	Positive Infinity	
1	111	0000	−Inf	Negative Infinity	Negative Infinity	
0/1	111	not zero	NaN	Not a Number	Not a Number	

11.9   DECODING THE DENORMALIZED REPRESENTATION

This small 8-bit floating-point format is especially useful in understanding the **denormalized** representation. Recall that the normalized representation simply does not provide a way to represent the floating-point value zero. The solution is to specify that if the biased exponent field is zero then the recreated hidden bit will be zero. Not only does the denormalized representation provide a way to encode the value zero, but it also provides a way to represent an additional set of small values. Here is an example of decoding a number using the denormalized interpretation:

```
1-bit  3-bit Biased  4-bit
Sign   Exponent      Significant
```

0	0	0	0	1	0	1	0

- The first bit indicates the sign of the number. (0: positive, 1: negative) For this example, we have a positive decimal number encoded.
- Subtract three from the value found in the biased exponent field to determine the actual exponent. For this example, the actual exponent is -3.
- Using the significand bits write the number in binary representation. In this case, the re-created hidden bit is 0. For this example, we have 0.1010×2^{-3}.
- Next, we shift the binary point three positions to the left as specified by the negative exponent. For our example, we now have 0.000101.

2^4	2^3	2^2	2^1	2^0	2^{-1}	2^{-2}	2^{-3}	2^{-4}	2^{-5}	2^{-6}
16	8	4	2	1	0.5	0.25	0.125	0.0625	0.03125	0.015625

- In the final step, we simply perform a binary to decimal conversion by evaluating the polynomial expansion of the binary number using the above table of values. For this example, we determine that 0.078125 is the equivalent decimal value. (0.0625 + 0.015625 = 0.078125)

11.10 UNDERFLOW AND OVERFLOW

Notice that 0.0078125 is the smallest value that can be represented in the small 8-bit floating-point representation. If we divide this value by two, we have no way to encode the result in our 8-bit representation. This is an example of **underflow**. By the same token, if we take the largest value 15.5 and multiply it by 2, we have no way to encode the result in our 8-bit representation. This is an example of **overflow**. This same problem exists for the IEEE floating-point formats, except that these situations arise with much smaller and much larger values at the extreme ranges of the IEEE floating-point formats. With the MIPS architecture, an exception is generated when either an underflow or an overflow occurs.

Final Words of Wisdom

Never fall in love with a tennis player.
Love means nothing to them.

Do you know how to make God laugh?
Tell him your plans.

EXERCISES

11.1 Write an interactive program that will convert input temperatures in Fahrenheit to Celsius. The program should prompt the user for a temperature in Fahrenheit and then print the corresponding temperature in Celsius. ($C = 5/9^*(F - 32)$)

11.2 Using Newton's method, develop a double-precision function that will return the square root of the positive double-precision floating-point value passed to the function. If the input argument is a negative value, return the value NaN.

11.3 This is an exercise in calling nested functions. Write a function to find the length of the hypotenuse of a right triangle whose sides are of length A and B. Write a main program to test this function.

11.4 This is an exercise in nested function calls and passing parameters on the stack. Write a function to calculate the roots of any quadratic equation of the form $y = ax^2 + bx + c$, where the floating-point values a, b, and c are passed to the function on the stack. Status, an integer value, should indicate the nature of the results returned as follows:

```
0 : 2 real roots R1 & R2
1 : 1 real root in R1= -a/b
2 : 2 complex roots of the form (R1 ± i R2)
3 : no roots computed (error)
```

11.5 Write a single-precision function that will convert an angle expressed in degrees to an angle expressed in radians. (radians = (degrees * π)/180)

11.6 In Section 10.8 of this chapter, a small 8-bit floating-point encoding was defined. Show the floating-point encoding for π and the square root of 2 in this small 8-bit floating-point representation. Approximately how inaccurate are these encoded values?

11.7 In Section 11.8 of this chapter, a small 8-bit floating-point representation was defined. Given this definition, the binary sequence 01000001 (0×41) represents the floating-point value $+1.0001 \times 2^1$, which is equivalent to $+2.125$ as a decimal number. It is interesting to note that 0×41 is the ASCII code for the letter A. (Check Appendix B.) Write a function that will print the decimal floating-point equivalent of any 8-bit value passed to it as an argument, using the floating-point interpretation rules presented in Section 11.8. Write a main program to test this function, where the source 8-bit values will be typed in as single keys on the keyboard.

11.8 Write a program that will generate and print NaN, positive infinity, and negative infinity. Include additional code to generate underflow and overflow to see what messages are produced when an exception occurs.

APPENDIX A

Quick Reference

INTEGER INSTRUCTION SET

Name	Syntax		Space/Time
Add	add	Rd, Rs, Rt	1/1
Add Immediate	addi	Rt, Rs, Imm	1/1
Add Immediate Unsigned	addiu	Rt, Rs, Imm	1/1
Add Unsigned	addu	Rd, Rs, Rt	1/1
And	and	Rd, Rs, Rt	1/1
And Immediate	andi	Rt, Rs, Imm	1/1
Branch if Equal	beq	Rs, Rt, Label	1/1
Branch if Greater Than or Equal to Zero	bgez	Rs, Label	1/1
Branch if Greater Than or Equal to Zero and Link	bgezal	Rs, Label	1/1
Branch if Greater Than Zero	bgtz	Rs, Label	1/1
Branch if Less Than or Equal to Zero	blez	Rs, Label	1/1
Branch if Less Than Zero and Link	bltzal	Rs, Label	1/1
Branch if Less Than Zero	bltz	Rs, Label	1/1
Branch if Not Equal	bne	Rs, Rt, Label	1/1
Divide	div	Rs, Rt	1/38
Divide Unsigned	divu	Rs, Rt	1/38
Jump	j	Label	1/1
Jump and Link	jal	Label	1/1
Jump and Link Register	jalr	Rd, Rs	1/1
Jump Register	jr	Rs	1/1
Load Byte	lb	Rt, offset(Rs)	1/1
Load Byte Unsigned	lbu	Rt, offset(Rs)	1/1
Load Halfword	lh	Rt, offset(Rs)	1/1
Load Halfword Unsigned	lhu	Rt, offset(Rs)	1/1
Load Upper Immediate	lui	Rt, Imm	1/1
Load Word	lw	Rt, offset(Rs)	1/1
Load Word Left	lwl	Rt, offset(Rs)	1/1
Load Word Right	lwr	Rt, offset(Rs)	1/1
Move From Coprocessor 0	mfc0	Rd, Cs	1/1
Move From High	mfhi	Rd	1/1
Move From Low	mflo	Rd	1/1

Move To Coprocessor 0	mtc0	Rt, Cd	1/1
Move to High	mthi	Rs	1/1
Move to Low	mtlo	Rs	1/1
Multiply	mult	Rs, Rt	1/32
Multiply Unsigned	multu	Rs, Rt	1/32
NOR	nor	Rd, Rs, Rt	1/1
OR	or	Rd, Rs, Rt	1/1
OR Immediate	ori	Rt, Rs, Imm	1/1
Return From Exception	rfe		1/1
Store Byte	sb	Rt, offset(Rs)	1/1
Store Halfword	sh	Rt, offset(Rs)	1/1
Shift Left Logical	sll	Rd, Rt, sa	1/1
Shift Left Logical Variable	sllv	Rd, Rt, Rs	1/1
Set on Less Than	slt	Rd, Rt, Rs	1/1
Set on Less Than Immediate	slti	Rt, Rs, Imm	1/1
Set on Less Than Immediate Unsigned	sltiu	Rt, Rs, Imm	1/1
Set on Less Than Unsigned	sltu	Rd, Rt, Rs	1/1
Shift Right Arithmetic	sra	Rd, Rt, sa	1/1
Shift Right Arithmetic Variable	srav	Rd, Rt, Rs	1/1
Shift Right Logical	srl	Rd, Rt, sa	1/1
Shift Right Logical Variable	srlv	Rd, Rt, Rs	1/1
Subtract	sub	Rd, Rs, Rt	1/1
Subtract Unsigned	subu	Rd, Rs, Rt	1/1
Store Word	sw	Rt, offset(Rs)	1/1
Store Word Left	swl	Rt, offset(Rs)	1/1
Store Word Right	swr	Rt, offset(Rs)	1/1
System Call	syscall		1/1
Exclusive OR	xor	Rd, Rs, Rt	1/1
Exclusive OR Immediate	xori	Rt, Rs, Imm	1/1

MACRO INSTRUCTIONS

Name	Syntax		Space/Time
Absolute Value	abs	Rd, Rs	3/3
Branch if Equal to Zero	beqz	Rs, Label	1/1
Branch if Greater Than or Equal	bge	Rs, Rt, Label	2/2
Branch if Greater Than or Equal Unsigned	bgeu	Rs, Rt, Label	2/2
Branch if Greater Than	bgt	Rs, Rt, Label	2/2
Branch if Greater Than Unsigned	bgtu	Rs, Rt, Label	2/2
Branch if Less Than or Equal	ble	Rs, Rt, Label	2/2
Branch if Less Than or Equal Unsigned	bleu	Rs, Rt, Label	2/2
Branch if Less Than	blt	Rs, Rt, Label	2/2
Branch if Less Than Unsigned	bltu	Rs, Rt, Label	2/2
Branch if Not Equal to Zero	bnez	Rs, Label	1/1
Branch Unconditional	b	Label	1/1
Divide	div	Rd, Rs, Rt	4/41
Divide Unsigned	divu	Rd, Rs, Rt	4/41
Load Address	la	Rd, Label	2/2
Load Immediate	li	Rd, value	2/2
Move	move	Rd, Rs	1/1
Multiply	mul	Rd, Rs, Rt	2/33
Multiply (with overflow exception)	mulo	Rd, Rs, Rt	7/37
Multiply Unsigned (with overflow exception)	mulou	Rd, Rs, Rt	5/35
Negate	neg	Rd, Rs	1/1

Negate Unsigned	negu	Rd, Rs	1/1
Nop	nop		1/1
Not	not	Rd, Rs	1/1
Remainder Unsigned	remu	Rd, Rs, Rt	4/40
Rotate Left Variable	rol	Rd, Rs, Rt	4/4
Rotate Right Variable	ror	Rd, Rs, Rt	4/4
Remainder	rem	Rd, Rs, Rt	4/40
Rotate Left Constant	rol	Rd, Rs, sa	3/3
Rotate Right Constant	ror	Rd, Rs, sa	3/3
Set if Equal	seq	Rd, Rs, Rt	4/4
Set if Greater Than or Equal	sge	Rd, Rs, Rt	4/4
Set if Greater Than or Equal Unsigned	sgeu	Rd, Rs, Rt	4/4
Set if Greater Than	sgt	Rd, Rs, Rt	1/1
Set if Greater Than Unsigned	sgtu	Rd, Rs, Rt	1/1
Set if Less Than or Equal	sle	Rd, Rs, Rt	4/4
Set if Less Than or Equal Unsigned	sleu	Rd, Rs, Rt	4/4
Set if Not Equal	sne	Rd, Rs, Rt	4/4
Unaligned Load Halfword Unsigned	ulh	Rd, n(Rs)	4/4
Unaligned Load Halfword	ulhu	Rd, n(Rs)	4/4
Unaligned Load Word	ulw	Rd, n(Rs)	2/2
Unaligned Store Halfword	ush	Rd, n(Rs)	3/3
Unaligned Store Word	usw	Rd, n(Rs)	2/2

SYSTEM I/O SERVICES

Service	Code in $v0	Argument(s)	Result(s)
Print Integer	1	$a0 = number to be printed	
Print Float	2	$f12 = number to be printed	
Print Double	3	$f12 = number to be printed	
Print String	4	$a0 = address of string in memory	
Read Integer	5		number returned in $v0
Read Float	6		number returned in $f0
Read Double	7		number returned in $f0
Read String	8	$a0 = address of input buffer in memory	
		$a1 = length of buffer (n)	
Sbrk	9	$a0 = amount	address in $v0
Exit	10		

The system call Read Integer reads an entire line of input from the keyboard up to and including the newline. Characters following the last digit in the decimal number are ignored. Read String has the same semantics as the Unix library routine fgets. It reads up to $n - 1$ characters into a buffer and terminates the string with a null byte. If fewer than $n - 1$ characters are on the current line, Read String reads up to and including the newline and again null terminates the string. Print String will display on the terminal the string of characters found in memory starting with the location pointed to by the address stored in $a0. Printing will stop when a null character is located in the string. Sbrk returns a pointer to a block of memory containing n additional bytes. Exit terminates the user program execution and returns control to the operating system.

ASSEMBLER DIRECTIVES

.align n	Align the next datum on a 2^n byte boundary. For example, .align 2 aligns the next value on a word boundary. .align 0 turns off automatic alignment of .half, .word, .float, and .double directives until the next .data or .kdata directive.
.ascii string*	Store the string in memory, but do not null-terminate it.
.asciiz string*	Store the string in memory and null-terminate it.
.byte b1,..., bn	Store the n 8-bit values in successive bytes of memory.
.data \<addr\>	Subsequent items are stored in the data segment. If the optional argument *addr* is present, subsequent items are stored starting at address *addr*. For example: .data 0x00008000
.double d1, ..., dn	Store the n floating-point double-precision numbers in successive memory locations.
.extern Symb size	Declare that the datum stored at *Symb* is of size bytes large and is a global label. This directive enables the assembler to store the datum in a portion of the data segment that is efficiently accessed via register $gp.
.float f1, ..., fn	Store the n floating-point single-precision numbers in successive memory locations.
.globl Symb	Declare that label *Symb* is global so it can be referenced from other files.
.half h1,... hn	Store the n 16-bit quantities in successive memory half words.
.kdata \<add\>	Subsequent items are stored in the kernel data segment. If the optional argument *addr* is present, subsequent items are stored starting at address *addr*.
.ktext \<addr\>	Subsequent items are put in the kernal text segment. In SPIM, these items may only be instructions or words. If the optional argument *addr* is present, subsequent items are stored starting at address *addr* (e.g., .ktext 0x80000080).
.space n	Allocate n bytes of space in the current segment (which must be the data segment in PCSpim).
.text \<addr\>	Subsequent items are put in the user text segment. In SPIM, these items may only be instructions or words (see the .word directive below). If the optional argument *addr* is present, subsequent items are stored starting at address *addr* (e.g., .data 0x00400000).
.word w1,..., wn	Store the n 32-bit quantities in successive memory words.
.word w : n	Stores the 32-bit value w into n successive memory words.

*Strings are enclosed in double quotes ("). Special characters in strings follow the C convention: newline: \n, tab: \t, quote: \". Instruction op-codes are reserved words and may not be used as labels. Labels must appear at the beginning of a line followed by a colon. The ASCII code "back space" is not supported by the SPIM simulator. Numbers are base 10 by default. If they are preceded by $0x$, they are interpreted as hexadecimal. Hence, 256 and 0x100 denote the same value.

APPENDIX B

ASCII Codes

dec	hex	Char	dec	hex	Char	dec	hex	Char	dec	hex	Char
0	00	nul	32	20	sp	64	40	@	96	60	'
1	01	soh	33	21	!	65	41	A	97	61	a
2	02	stx	34	22	"	66	42	B	98	62	b
3	03	etx	35	23	#	67	43	C	99	63	c
4	04	eot	36	24	$	68	44	D	100	64	d
5	05	enq	37	25	%	69	45	E	101	65	e
6	06	ack	38	26	&	70	46	F	102	66	f
7	07	bel	39	27	'	71	47	G	103	67	g
8	08	bs	40	28	(	72	48	H	104	68	h
9	09	ht	41	29	)	73	49	I	105	69	i
10	0a	nl	42	2a	*	74	4a	J	106	6a	j
11	0b	vt	43	2b	+	75	4b	K	107	6b	k
12	0c	np	44	2c	,	76	4c	L	108	6c	l
13	0d	cr	45	2d	−	77	4d	M	109	6d	m
14	0e	so	46	2e	.	78	4e	N	110	6e	n
15	0f	si	47	2f	/	79	4f	O	111	6f	o
16	10	dle	48	30	0	80	50	P	112	70	p
17	11	dc1	49	31	1	81	51	Q	113	71	q
18	12	dc2	50	32	2	82	52	R	114	72	r
19	13	dc3	51	33	3	83	53	S	115	73	s
20	14	dc4	52	34	4	84	54	T	116	74	t
21	15	nak	53	35	5	85	55	U	117	75	u
22	16	syn	54	36	6	86	56	V	118	76	v
23	17	etb	55	37	7	87	57	W	119	77	w
24	18	can	56	38	8	88	58	X	120	78	x
25	19	em	57	39	9	89	59	Y	121	79	y
26	1a	sub	58	3a	:	90	5a	Z	122	7a	z
27	1b	esc	59	3b	;	91	5b	[	123	7b	{
28	1c	fs	60	3c	<	92	5c	\	124	7c		
29	1d	gs	61	3d	=	93	5d	]	125	7d	}
30	1e	rs	62	3e	>	94	5e	^	126	7e	~
31	1f	us	63	3f	?	95	5f	_	127	7f	del

APPENDIX C

Integer Instruction Set

Add

add   Rd, Rs, Rt   # RF[Rd] = RF[Rs] + RF[Rt]

Op-Code	Rs	Rt	Rd	Function Code
000000	sssss	ttttt	ddddd	00000 100000

Add contents of Reg.File[Rs] to Reg.File[Rt] and store result in Reg.File[Rd]. If overflow occurs in the two's complement number system, an exception is generated.

Add Immediate

addi   Rt, Rs, Imm   # RF[Rt] = RF[Rs] + se Imm

Op-Code	Rs	Rt	Imm
001000	sssss	ttttt	iiiiiiiiiiiiiiii

Add contents of Reg.File[Rs] to sign extended (se) Imm value; store result in Reg.File [Rt]. If overflow occurs in the two's complement number system, an exception is generated.

Add Immediate Unsigned

addiu Rt, Rs, Imm   # RF[Rt] = RF[Rs] + se Imm

Op-Code	Rs	Rt	Imm
001001	sssss	ttttt	iiiiiiiiiiiiiiii

Add contents of Reg.File[Rs] to sign extended (se) Imm value; store result in Reg. File[Rt]. No overflow exception is generated.

Add Unsigned

addu Rd, Rs, Rt   # RF[Rd] = RF[Rs] + RF[Rt]

Op-Code	Rs	Rt	Rd	Function Code
000000	sssss	ttttt	ddddd	00000	100001

Add contents of Reg.File[Rs] to Reg.File[Rt] and store result in Reg.File [Rd]. No overflow exception is generated.

And

and Rd, Rs, Rt   # RF[Rd] = RF[Rs] AND RF[Rt]

Op-Code	Rs	Rt	Rd	Function Code
000000	sssss	ttttt	ddddd	00000	100100

Bitwise logically AND contents of Reg.File[Rs] with Reg.File[Rt] and store result in Reg.File[Rd].

And Immediate

andi Rt, Rs, Imm   # RF[Rt] = RF[Rs] AND ze Imm

Op-Code	Rs	Rt	Imm
001100	sssss	ttttt	iiiiiiiiiiiiiiii

Bitwise logically AND contents of Reg.File[Rs] wih zero-extended (ze) Imm value and store result in Reg.File[Rt].

Branch Instructions

The immediate field contains a signed 16-bit value specifying the number of words away from the current program counter address to the location symbolically specified by the label. Since MIPS uses byte addressing, this word offset value in the immediate field is shifted left by 2 bits, which accomplishes a multiply by 4, and added to the current contents of the program counter when a branch is taken. The SPIM assembler generates the offset from the address of the branch instruction. Whereas the assembler for an actual MIPS processor will generate the offset from the address of the instruction following the branch instruction since the program counter will have already been incremented by the time the branch instruction is executed.

Branch if Equal

beq Rs, Rt, Label   # If (RF[Rs] == RF[Rt])then PC = PC + se Imm<< 2

Op-Code	Rs	Rt	Imm
000100	sssss	ttttt	iiiiiiiiiiiiiiii

If Reg.File[Rs] is equal to Reg.File[Rt] then branch to label.

Branch if Greater Than or Equal to Zero

bgez Rs, Label   # If (RF[Rs] >= RF[0]) then PC = PC + se Imm<< 2

Op-Code	Rs	code	Imm

```
000001 sssss 00001 iiiiiiiiiiiiiiii
```

If Reg.File[Rs] is greater than or equal to zero, then branch to label.

Branch if Greater Than or Equal to Zero and Link

bgezal Rs, Label   # If(RF[Rs] >= RF[0])then
                                                     {RF[$ra] = PC;
                                                     PC = PC + se Imm << 2 }

Op-Code	Rs	code	Imm

```
000001 sssss 10001 iiiiiiiiiiiiiiii
```

If Reg.File[Rs] is greater than or equal to zero, then save the return address in Reg.File[$rs] and branch to label (used to make conditional function calls).

Branch if Greater Than Zero

bgtz Rs, Label   # If (RF[Rs] > RF[0]) then PC = PC + se Imm << 2

Op-Code	Rs	Rt	Imm

```
000111 sssss 00000 iiiiiiiiiiiiiiii
```

If Reg.File[Rs] is greater than zero, then branch to label.

Branch if Less Than or Equal to Zero

blez Rs, Label   # If (RF[Rs] <= RF[0]) then PC = PC + se Imm << 2

Op-Code	Rs	Rt	Imm

```
000110 sssss 00000 iiiiiiiiiiiiiiii
```

If Reg.File[Rs] is less than or equal to zero, then branch to label.

Branch if Less Than Zero and Link

bltzal Rs, Label   # If RF[Rs] < RF[0] then
                                                     {RF[$ra] = PC;
                                                     PC = PC + se Imm << 2 }

Op-Code	Rs	code	Imm

```
000001 sssss 10000 iiiiiiiiiiiiiiii
```

If Reg.File[Rs] is less than zero then save the return address in Reg.File[$rs] and branch to label.

Branch if Less Than Zero

bltz   Rs, Label   # If RF[Rs] < RF[0] then PC = PC + se Imm << 2

Op-Code	Rs	code	Imm
000001	sssss	00000	iiiiiiiiiiiiiiii

If Reg.File[Rs] is less than zero then branch to label.

Branch if Not Equal

bne   Rs, Rt, Label   # If RF[Rs] != RF[Rt] then PC = PC + se Imm << 2

Op-Code	Rs	Rt	Imm
000101	sssss	ttttt	iiiiiiiiiiiiiiii

If Reg.File[Rs] is not equal to Reg.File[Rt] then branch to label.

Divide

div   Rs, Rt   # LOW = Quotient (RF[Rs] / RF[Rt])
                                    # HIGH = Remainder (RF[Rs] / RF[Rt])

Op-Code	Rs	Rt			Function Code
000000	sssss	ttttt	00000	00000	011010

Divide the contents of Reg.File[Rs] by Reg.File[Rt]. Store the quotient in the LOW register, and store the remainder in the HIGH register. The sign of the quotient will be negative if the operands are of opposite signs. The sign of the remainder will be the same as the sign of the numerator, Reg.File[Rs]. No overflow exception occurs under any circumstances. It is the programmer's responsibility to test if the divisor is zero before executing this instruction, because the results are undefined when the divisor is zero. For some implementations of the MIPS architecture, it takes 38 clock cycles to execute the divide instruction.

Divide Unsigned

divu Rs, Rt   # LOW = Quotient (RF[Rs] / RF[Rt])
                                    # HIGH = Remainder (RF[Rs] / RF[Rt])

Op-Code	Rs	Rt			Function Code
000000	sssss	ttttt	00000	00000	011011

Divide the contents of Reg.File[Rs] by Reg.File[Rt], treating both operands as unsigned values. Store the quotient in the LOW register, and store the remainder in the HIGH register. The quotient and remainder will always be positive values. No overflow exception occurs under any circumstances. It is the programmer's responsibility to test if the divisor is zero before executing this instruction, because the results are undefined when the divisor is zero. For some implementations of the MIPS architecture, it takes 38 clock cycles to execute the divide instruction.

Jump

j   Label   # PC = PC(31:28) | Imm << 2

Op-Code   Imm
`000010iiiiiiiiiiiiiiiiiiiiiiiiii`

Load the PC with an address formed by concatenating the first 4 bits of the current PC with the value in the 26-bit immediate field shifted left 2 bits.

Jump and Link   (Use this instruction to make function calls.)

jal   Label   # RF[$ra] = PC; PC = PC(31:28) | Imm << 2

Op-Code   Imm
`000010iiiiiiiiiiiiiiiiiiiiiiiiii`

Save the current value of the PC in Reg.File[$ra], and load the PC with an address formed by concatenating the first 4 bits of the current PC with the value in the 26-bit immediate field shifted left 2 bits.

Jump and Link Register

jalr   Rd, Rs   # RF[Rd] = PC; PC = RF[Rs]

			Function
Op-Code	Rs	Rd	Code

`000000sssss00000ddddd00000001001`

Save the current value of the program counter in Reg.File[Rd] and load the program counter with the address that is in Reg.File[Rs]. A programmer must ensure a valid address has been loaded into Reg.File[Rs] before executing this instruction. (This instruction is frequently used to make function calls.)

Jump Register

jr   Rs   # PC = RF[Rs]

		Function
Op-Code	Rs	Code

`000000sssss000000000000000001000`

Load the program counter with the address that is in Reg.File[Rs]. (This instruction is frequently used to return from a function call.)

Load Byte

lb   Rt, offset(Rs)   # RF[Rt] = se (Mem[RF[Rs] + se Offset])

Op-Code	Rs	Rt	Offset
100000	sssss	ttttt	iiiiiiiiiiiiiiii

The 16-bit offset is sign extended and added to Reg.File[Rs] to form an effective address. An 8-bit byte is read from memory at the effective address, sign extended, and loaded into Reg.File[Rt].

Load Byte Unsigned

lbu   Rt, offset(Rs)   # RF[Rt] = ze (Mem[RF[Rs] + se Offset])

Op-Code	Rs	Rt	Offset
100100	sssss	ttttt	iiiiiiiiiiiiiiii

The 16-bit offset is sign extended and added to Reg.File[Rs] to form an effective address. An 8-bit byte is read from memory at the effective address, zero extended, and loaded into Reg.File[Rt]. This is an unsigned type of instruction because the data read from memory is zero extended.

Load Halfword

lh   Rt, offset(Rs)   # RF[Rt] = se (Mem[RF[Rs] + se Offset])

Op-Code	Rs	Rt	Offset
100001	sssss	ttttt	iiiiiiiiiiiiiiii

The 16-bit offset is sign extended and added to Reg.File[Rs] to form an effective address. A 16-bit half word is read from memory at the effective address, sign extended, and loaded into Reg.File[Rt]. If the effective address is an odd number, an address error exception occurs.

Load Halfword Unsigned

lhu   Rt, offset(Rs)   # RF[Rt] = ze (Mem[RF[Rs] + se Offset])

Op-Code	Rs	Rt	Offset
100101	sssss	ttttt	iiiiiiiiiiiiiiii

The 16-bit offset is sign extended and added to Reg.File[Rs] to form an effective address. A 16-bit half word is read from memory at the effective address, zero extended, and loaded into Reg.File[Rt]. If the effective address is an odd number, an address error exception occurs. This is an unsigned type of instruction because the data read from memory is zero extended.

Load Upper Immediate

lui   Rt, Imm   # RF[Rt] = Imm <<16 | 0x0000

Op-Code   Rt   Imm
`001111 00000 ttttt iiiiiiiiiiiiiiii`

The 16-bit immediate value is shifted left 16 bits concatenated with 16 zeros and loaded into Reg.File[Rt]. This instruction in conjunction with an OR immediate instruction is used to implement the Load Address pseudo instruction, la Label.

Load Word

lw   Rt, offset(Rs)   # RF[Rt] = Mem[RF[Rs] + se Offset]

Op-Code   Rs   Rt   Offset
`100011 sssss ttttt iiiiiiiiiiiiiiii`

The 16-bit offset is sign extended and added to Reg.File[Rs] to form an effective address. A 32-bit word is read from memory at the effective address and loaded into Reg.File[Rt]. If the least 2 significant bits of the effective address are not zero, an address error exception occurs. There are 4 bytes in a word, so word addresses must be binary numbers that are a multiple of four, otherwise an address error exception occurs.

Load Word Left

lwl   Rt, offset(Rs)   # RF[Rt] = Mem[RF[Rs] + se Offset]

Op-Code   Rs   Rt   Offset
`100010 sssss ttttt iiiiiiiiiiiiiiii`

The 16-bit offset is sign extended and added to Reg.File[Rs] to form an effective byte address. From 1 to 4 bytes will be loaded left justified into Reg.File[Rt], beginning with the effective byte address. Then it proceeds toward a lower order byte in memory, until it reaches the lowest-order byte of the word in memory. This instruction can be used in combination with the LWR instruction to load a register with 4 consecutive bytes from memory, when the bytes cross a boundary between two words.

Load Word Right

lwr   Rt, offset(Rs)   # RF[Rt] = Mem[RF[Rs] + se Offset]

Op-Code   Rs   Rt   Offset
`100110 sssss ttttt iiiiiiiiiiiiiiii`

The 16-bit offset is sign extended and added to Reg.File[Rs] to form an effective byte address. From 1 to 4 bytes will be loaded right justified into Reg.File[Rt], beginning with the effective byte address. Then it proceeds toward a higher order byte in memory, until it reaches the high-order byte of the word in memory. This instruction can be used in combination with the LWL instruction to load a register with 4 consecutive bytes from memory, when the bytes cross a boundary between 2 words.

Move From Coprocessor 0

mfc0   Rt, Cd   # RF[Rt] = Cs

Op-Code		Rt	Cs		
010000	00000	ttttt	ddddd	00000	000000

Load Reg.File[Rt] with a copy of the value currently in specified coprocessor register. Used to process exceptions. For example, mfc0 $k0, $13 will load register $k0 with a copy of the cause register. This instruction is used when processing exceptions.

Move From High

mfhi   Rd   # RF[Rd] = HIGH

Op-Code			Rd	Function Code	
000000	00000	00000	ddddd	00000	010000

Load Reg.File[Rd] with a copy of the value currently in special register HIGH.

Move From Low

mflo   Rd   # RF[Rd] = LOW

Op-Code			Rd	Function Code	
000000	00000	00000	ddddd	00000	010010

Load Reg.File[Rd] with a copy of the value currently in special register LOW.

Move to Coprocessor 0 Register

mtco   Rs, Cd   # Cd = RF[Rt]

Op-Code		Rt	Cd		
010000	00100	ttttt	ddddd	00000	000000

Load specified coprocessor register with a copy of the value currently in Rs. Notice that this is the only MIPS instruction that specifies the destination on the right side. Used to process exceptions. For example, mtc0 $0, $13 will clear the cause register.

Move To High

mthi Rs   # HIGH = RF[Rs]

Op-Code	Rs			Function Code
000000	sssss	00000	00000 00000	010001

Load special register HIGH with a copy of the value currently in Reg.File[Rs].

Move To Low

mtlo Rs   # LOW = RF[Rs]

Op-Code	Rs			Function Code
000000	sssss	00000	00000 00000	010011

Load special register LOW with a copy of the value currently in Reg.File[Rs].

Multiply

mult Rs, Rt   # HIGH |LOW = RF[Rs] * RF[Rt]

Op-Code	Rs	Rt		Function Code
000000	sssss	ttttt	00000 00000	011000

Multiply the contents of Reg.File[Rs] by Reg.File[Rt] and store the lower 32 bits of the product in the LOW register, and store the upper 32 bits of the product in the HIGH register. The two operands are treated as two's complement numbers; the 64-bit product is negative if the signs of the two operands are different. No overflow exception occurs under any circumstances. For some implementations of the MIPS architecture, it takes 32 clock cycles to execute the multiply instruction.

Multiply Unsigned

multu Rs, Rt   # HIGH |LOW = RF[Rs] * RF[Rt]

Op-Code	Rs	Rt		Function Code
000000	sssss	ttttt	00000 00000	011001

Multiply the contents of Reg.File[Rs] by Reg.File[Rt] and store the lower 32 bits of the product in the LOW register, and store the upper 32 bits of the product in the HIGH register. The two operands are treated as unsigned positive values. No overflow exception occurs under any circumstances. For some implementations of the MIPS architecture, it takes 32 clock cycles to execute the multiply instruction.

NOR

nor Rd, Rs, Rt   # RF[Rd] = RF[Rs] NOR RF[Rt]

Op-Code	Rs	Rt	Rd		Function Code
000000	sssss	ttttt	ddddd	00000	100111

Bitwise logically NOR contents of Register File[Rs] with Reg.File[Rt] and store result in Reg.File[Rd].

OR

or Rd, Rs, Rt   # RF[Rd] = RF[Rs] OR RF[Rt]

Op-Code	Rs	Rt	Rd		Function Code
000000	sssss	ttttt	ddddd	00000	100101

Bitwise logically OR contents of Reg.File[Rs] with Reg.File[Rt] and store result in Reg.File[Rd].

OR Immediate

ori   Rt, Rs, Imm   # RF[Rt] = RF[Rs] OR Imm

Op-Code	Rs	Rt	Imm
001101	sssss	ttttt	iiiiiiiiiiiiiiii

Bitwise logically OR contents of Reg.File[Rs] with zero-extended Imm value and store result in Reg.File[Rt].

Return From Exception

rfe

Op-Code				Function Code
010000	00000	00000	000000000	100000

Restore the status register to the value it contained before the last exception occurred.

Store Byte

sb   Rt, offset(Rs)   # Mem[RF[Rs] + se Offset] = RF[Rt]

Op-Code	Rs	Rt	Offset
101000	sssss	ttttt	iiiiiiiiiiiiiiii

The 16-bit offset is sign extended and added to Reg.File[Rs] to form an effective address. The least significant 8-bit byte in Reg.File[Rt] is stored in memory at the effective address.

Store Halfword

sh   Rt, offset(Rs)   # Mem[RF[Rs] + se Offset] = RF[Rt]

Op-Code	Rs	Rt	Offset
101001	sssss	ttttt	iiiiiiiiiiiiiiii

The 16-bit offset is sign extended and added to Reg.File[Rs] to form an effective address. The least significant 16 bits in Reg.File[Rt] are stored in memory at the effective address. If the effective address is an odd number, then an address error exception occurs.

Shift Left Logical

sll   Rd, Rt, sa   # RF[Rd] = RF[Rt] << sa

Op-Code		Rt	Rd	sa	Function Code
000000	00000	ttttt	ddddd	iiiii	000000

The contents of Reg.File[Rt] are shifted left sa bits, and the result is stored in Reg.File[Rd].

Shift Left Logical Variable

sllv   Rd, Rt, Rs   # RF[Rd] = RF[Rt] << RF[Rs] amount

Op-Code	Rs	Rt	Rd		Function Code
000000	sssss	ttttt	ddddd	00000	000100

The contents of Reg.File[Rt] are shifted left by the number of bits specified by the low-order 5 bits of Reg.File[Rs], and the result is stored in Reg.File[Rd].

Set on Less Than

slt   Rd, Rs, Rt # if (RF[Rs] < se RF[Rt]) then RF[Rd] = 1 else RF[Rd] = 0

Op-Code	Rs	Rt	Rd		Function Code
000000	sssss	ttttt	ddddd	00000	101010

If the contents of Reg.File[Rs] are less than the contents of Reg.File[Rt], then Reg.File[Rd] is set to one, otherwise Reg.File[Rd] is set to zero, assuming the two's complement number system representation (used in branch macro instructions).

Set on Less Than Immediate

slti   Rt, Rs, Imm   # if (RF[Rs] < se Imm) then RF[Rt] = 1 else RF[Rt] = 0

Op-Code	Rs	Rt	Imm
001010	sssss	ttttt	iiiiiiiiiiiiiiii

If the contents of Reg.File[Rs] are less than the sign-extended immediate value then Reg.File[Rt] is set to one; otherwise Reg.File[Rt] is set to zero, assuming the two's complement number system representation (used in branch macro instructions).

Set on Less Than Immediate Unsigned

sltiu Rt, Rs, Imm   # if (RF[Rs] < ze Imm) then RF[Rt] = 1 else RF[Rt] = 0

Op-Code	Rs	Rt	Imm
001011	sssss	ttttt	iiiiiiiiiiiiiiii

If the contents of Reg.File[Rs] are less than the sign-extended immediate value, then Reg.File[Rt] is set to one; otherwise Reg.File[Rt] is set to zero. This assumes an unsigned number representation (only positive values).

Set on Less Than Unsigned

sltu   Rd, Rs, Rt   # if (RF[Rs] < RF[Rt]) then RF[Rd] = 1 else RF[Rd] = 0

Op-Code	Rs	Rt	Rd		Function Code
000000	sssss	ttttt	ddddd	00000	101010

If the contents of Reg.File[Rs] are less than the contents of Reg.File[Rt], then Reg.File[Rd] is set to one, otherwise Reg.File[Rd] is set to zero. This assumes an unsigned number representation (only positive values).

Shift Right Arithmetic

sra   Rd, Rt, sa # RF[Rd] = RF[Rt] > sa

Op-Code		Rt	Rd	sa	Function Code
000000	00000	ttttt	ddddd	iiiii	000011

The contents of Reg.File[Rt] are shifted right sa bits, sign-extending the high-order bits, and the result is stored in Reg.File[Rd].

Shift Right Arithmetic Variable

srav Rd, Rt, Rs   # RF[Rd] = RF[Rt] > RF[Rs]

Op-Code	Rs	Rt	Rd		Function Code
000000	sssss	ttttt	ddddd	00000	000111

The contents of Reg.File[Rt] are shifted right, sign-extending the high-order bits by the number of bits specified by the low-order 5 bits of Reg.File[Rs], and the result is stored in Reg.File[Rd].

Shift Right Logical

srl   Rd, Rt, sa   # RF[Rd] = RF[Rt] > sa

Op-Code		Rt	Rd	sa	Function Code
000000	00000	ttttt	ddddd	iiiii	000010

The contents of Reg.File[Rt] are shifted right sa bits, inserting zeros into the high-order bits. The result is stored in Reg.File[Rd].

Shift Right Logical Variable

srlv   Rd, Rt, Rs   # RF[Rd] = RF[Rt] > RF[Rs] amount

Op-Code	Rs	Rt	Rd		Function Code
000000	sssss	ttttt	ddddd	00000	000110

The contents of Reg.File[Rt] are shifted right, inserting zeros into the high-order bits, by the number of bits specified by the low-order 5 bits of Reg.File[Rs], and the result is stored in Reg.File[Rd].

Subtract

sub   Rd, Rs, Rt   # RF[Rd] = RF[Rs] − RF[Rt]

Op-Code	Rs	Rt	Rd		Function Code
000000	sssss	ttttt	ddddd	00000	100010

Subtract contents of Reg.File[Rt] from Reg.File[Rs] and store result in Reg.File[Rd]. If overflow occurs in the two's complement number system, an exception is generated.

Subtract Unsigned

subu Rd, Rs, Rt   # RF[Rd] = RF[Rs] − RF[Rt]

Op-Code	Rs	Rt	Rd		Function Code
000000	sssss	ttttt	ddddd	00000	100011

Subtract contents of Reg.File[Rt] from Reg.File[Rs] and store result in Reg.File[Rd]. No overflow exception is generated.

Store Word

sw   Rt, offset(Rs)   # Mem[RF[Rs] + se Offset] = RF[Rt]

Op-Code	Rs	Rt	Offset
101011	sssss	ttttt	iiiiiiiiiiiiiiii

The 16-bit offset is sign extended and added to Reg.File[Rs] to form an effective address. The contents of Reg.File[Rt] are stored in memory at the effective address. If the least 2 significant bits of the effective address are not zero, an address error exception occurs. There are 4 bytes in a word, so word addresses must be binary numbers that are a multiple of 4, otherwise an address error exception occurs.

Store Word Left

swl   Rt, offset(Rs)   # Mem[RF[Rs] + se Offset] = RF[Rt]

Op-Code	Rs	Rt	Offset
101010	sssss	ttttt	iiiiiiiiiiiiiiii

The 16-bit offset is sign extended and added to Reg.File[Rs] to form an effective address. From 1 to 4 bytes will be stored left justified into memory, beginning with the most significant byte in Reg.File[Rt]. Then it proceeds toward a lower order byte in memory, until it reaches the lowest-order byte of the word in memory. This instruction can be used in combination with the SWR instruction to store the contents of a register into 4 consecutive bytes of memory when the bytes cross a boundary between two words.

Store Word Right

swr   Rt, offset(Rs)   # Mem[RF[Rs] + se Offset] = RF[Rt]

Op-Code	Rs	Rt	Offset
101110	sssss	ttttt	iiiiiiiiiiiiiiii

The 16-bit offset is sign extended and added to Reg.File[Rs] to form an effective address. From 1 to 4 bytes will be stored right justified into memory, beginning with the least significant byte in Reg.File[Rt]. Then it proceeds toward a higher order byte in memory, until it reaches the highest-order byte of the word in memory. This instruction can be used in combination with the SWL instruction to store the contents of a register into 4 consecutive bytes of memory when the bytes cross a boundary between two words.

System Call (used to call system services to perform I/O)

syscall

Op-Code				Function Code
000000	00000	00000	00000000	001100

A user program exception is generated

Exclusive OR

xor Rd, Rs, Rt   # RF[Rd] = RF[Rs] XOR RF[Rt]

Op-Code	Rs	Rt	Rd	Function Code

`000000ssssstttttddddd00000100110`

Bitwise logically Exclusive-OR contents of Register File[Rs] with Reg.File[Rt] and store result in Reg.File[Rd].

Exclusive OR Immediate

xori Rt, Rs, Imm   # RF[Rt] = RF[Rs] XOR ze Imm

Op-Code	Rs	Rt	Imm

`001110ssssstttttiiiiiiiiiiiiiiii`

Bitwise logically Exclusive-OR contents of Reg.File[Rs] with zero extended immediate value and store result in Reg.File[Rt].

Macro Instructions

Name	Actual Code	Space/Time

Absolute Value:
abs Rd, Rs
	addu Rd, $0, Rs
	bgez Rs, 1
	sub Rd, $0, Rs
		3/3

Branch if Equal to Zero: **beqz Rs, Label**	beq Rs, $0, Label	1/1
Branch if Greater than or Equal: **bge Rs, Rt, Label**	slt $at, Rs, Rt beq $at, $0, Label	2/2

If Reg.File[Rs] > = Reg.File[Rt] branch to Label
Used to compare values represented in the two's complement number system.

Branch if Greater than or Equal Unsigned **bgeu Rs, Rt, Label**	sltu $at, Rs, Rt beq $at, $0, Label	2/2

If Reg.File[Rs] > = Reg.File[Rt] branch to Label
Used to compare addresses (unsigned values).

Branch if Greater Than: **bgt Rs, Rt, Label**	slt $at, Rt, Rs bne $at, $0, Label	2/2

If Reg.File[Rs] > Reg.File[Rt] branch to Label
Used to compare values represented in the two's complement number system.

Branch if Greater Than Unsigned: **bgtu Rs, Rt, Label**	sltu $at, Rt, Rs bne $at, $0, Label	2/2

If Reg.File[Rs] > Reg.File[Rt] branch to Label
Used to compare addresses (unsigned values).

Branch if Less Than or Equal: **ble Rs, Rt, Label**	slt $at, Rt, Rs beq $at, $0, Label	2/2

If Reg.File[Rs] < = Reg.File[Rt] branch to Label
Used to compare values represented in the two's complement number system.

Branch if Less Than or Equal Unsigned:
  bleu Rs, Rt, Label

sltu $at, Rt, Rs
beq $at, $0, Label

2/2

If Reg.File[Rs] < = Reg.File[Rt] branch to Label
Used to compare addresses (unsigned values).

Branch if Less Than:
  blt Rs, Rt, Label

slt $at, Rs, Rt
bne $at, $0, Label

2/2

If Reg.File[Rs] < Reg.File[Rt] branch to Label
Used to compare values represented in the two's complement number system.

Branch if Less Than Unsigned:
  bltu Rs, Rt, Label

sltu $at, Rs, Rt
bne $at, $0, Label

2/2

If Reg.File[Rs] < Reg.File[Rt] branch to Label
Used to compare addresses (unsigned values).

Branch if Not Equal to Zero:
  bnez Rs, Label

bne Rs, $0, Label

1/1

Branch Unconditional
  b Label

bgez $0, Label

1/1

Divide:
  div Rd, Rs, Rt

bne Rt, $0, ok
break $0
ok: div Rs, Rt
mflo Rd

4/41

Divide Unsigned:
  divu Rd, Rs, Rt

bne Rt, $0, ok
break $0
ok: divu Rs, Rt
mflo Rd

4/41

Load Address:
  la Rd, Label

lui $at, Upper 16-bits of Label
ori Rd, $at, Lower 16-bits of Label

2/2

Used to initialize pointers.

Load Immediate:
  li Rd, value

lui $at, Upper 16-bits of value
ori Rd, $at, Lower 16-bits of value

2/2

Initialize registers with negative constants and values greater than 32,767.

Load Immediate:
  li Rd, value

ori Rt, $0, value

1/1

Initialize registers with positive constants less than 32,768.

Move:
  move Rd, Rs

addu Rd, $0, Rs

1/1

  mul Rd, Rs, Rt

mult Rs, Rt
mflo Rd

2/33

Multiply (with overflow exception):
  mulo Rd, Rs, Rt

mult Rs, Rt
mfhi $at
mflo Rd
sra Rd, Rd, 31
beq $at, Rd, ok

7/37

	break $0	
ok:	mflo Rd	

Multiply Unsigned (with overflow exception):
mulou Rd, Rs, Rt

	multu Rs, Rt	**5/35**
	mfhi $at	
	beq $at, $0, ok	
ok:	break $0	
	mflo Rd	

Negate:
neg Rd, Rs   sub Rd, $0, Rs   **1/1**

Two's complement negation. An exception is generated when there is an attempt to negate the most negative value: $-2{,}147{,}483{,}648$.

Negate Unsigned:
negu Rd, Rs   subu Rd, $0, Rs   **1/1**

Nop:
nop   or $0, $0, $0   **1/1**

Used to solve problems with hazards in the pipeline.

Not:
not Rd, Rs   nor Rd, Rs, $0   **1/1**

A bitwise Boolean complement.

Remainder:
rem Rd, Rs, Rt

bne Rt, $0, 8		**4/40**
break $0		
div Rs, Rt		
mfhi Rd		

Remainder Unsigned:
remu Rd, Rs, Rt

	bne Rt, $0, ok	**4/40**
	break $0	
ok:	divu Rs, Rt	
	mfhi Rd	

Rotate Left Variable:
rol Rd, Rs, Rt

subu $at, $0, Rt	**4/4**
srlv $at, Rs, $at	
sllv Rd, Rs, Rt	
or Rd, Rd, $at	

The lower 5 bits in Rt specify the shift amount.

Rotate Right Variable:
ror Rd, Rs, Rt

subu $at, $0, Rt	**4/4**
sllv $at, Rs, $at	
srlv Rd, Rs, Rt	
or Rd, Rd, $at	

Rotate Left Constant:
rol Rd, Rs, sa

srl $at, Rs, 32-sa	**3/3**
sll Rd, Rs, sa	
or Rd, Rd, $at	

Rotate Right Constant:
ror Rd, Rs, sa   sll $at, Rs, 32-sa   **3/3**

srl Rd, Rs, sa
or Rd, Rd, $at

Set if Equal:
  seq Rd, Rs, Rt

beq Rt, Rs, yes   4/4
ori Rd, $0, 0
beq $0, $0, skip
yes: ori Rd, $0, 1
skip:

Set if Greater Than or Equal:
  sge Rd, Rs, Rt

bne Rt, Rs, yes   4/4
ori Rd, $0, 1
beq $0, $0, skip
yes: slt Rd, Rt, Rs
skip:

Set if Greater Than or Equal Unsigned:
  sgeu Rd, Rs, Rt

bne Rt, Rs, yes   4/4
ori Rd, $0, 1
beq $0, $0, skip
yes: sltu Rd, Rt, Rs
skip:

Set if Greater Than:
  sgt Rd, Rs, Rt

slt Rd, Rt, Rs   1/1

Set if Greater Than Unsigned:
  sgtu Rd, Rs, Rt

sltu Rd, Rt, Rs   1/1

Set if Less Than or Equal:
  sle Rd, Rs, Rt

bne Rt, Rs, yes   4/4
ori Rd, $0, 1
beq $0, $0, skip
yes: slt Rd, Rs, Rt
skip:

Set if Less Than or Equal Unsigned:
  sleu Rd, Rs, Rt

bne Rt, Rs, yes   4/4
ori Rd, $0, 1
beq $0, $0, skip
yes: sltu Rd, Rs, Rt
skip:

Set if Not Equal:
  sne Rd, Rs, Rt

beq Rt, Rs, yes   4/4
ori Rd, $0, 1
beq $0, $0, skip
yes: ori Rd, $0, 0
skip:

Unaligned Load Halfword Unsigned:
  ulh Rd, 3(Rs)

lb Rd, 4(Rs)   4/4
lbu $at, 3(Rs)
sll Rd, Rd, 8
or Rd, Rd, $at

Unaligned Load Halfword:		
ulhu Rd, 3(Rs)	lbu Rd, 4(Rs)	4/4
	lbu $at, 3(Rs)	
	sll Rd, Rd, 8	
	or Rd, Rd, $at	
Unaligned Load Word:		
ulw Rd, 3(Rs)	lwl Rd, 6(Rs)	2/2
	lwr Rd, 3(Rs)	
Unaligned Store Halfword:		
ush Rd, 3(Rs)	sb Rd, 3(Rs)	3/3
	srl $at, Rd, 8	
	sb $at, 4(Rs)	
Unaligned Store Word:		
usw Rd, 3(Rs)	swl Rd, 6(Rs)	2/2
	swr Rd, 3(Rs)	

A P P E N D I X   E

A Modified Trap Handler

```
################################################################
# SPIM S20 MIPS simulator.
# A modified trap handler that responds to keyboard interrupts
################################################################
# Copyright (C) 1990-2000 James Larus, larus@cs.wisc.edu.
# ALL RIGHTS RESERVED.
#
# SPIM is distributed under the following conditions:
#
# You may make copies of SPIM for your own use and modify those copies.
#
# All copies of SPIM must retain my name and copyright notice.
#
# You may not sell SPIM or distributed SPIM in conjunction with a
# commercial product or service without the expressed written
# consent of James Larus.
#
# THIS SOFTWARE IS PROVIDED ``AS IS'' AND WITHOUT ANY EXPRESS OR
# IMPLIED WARRANTIES, INCLUDING, WITHOUT LIMITATION, THE IMPLIED
# WARRANTIES OF MERCHANTABILITY AND FITNESS FOR A PARTICULAR
# PURPOSE.
################################################################
```

```
            .kdata
__m1__:     .asciiz "  Exception "
__m2__:     .asciiz " occurred and ignored\n"
__e0__:     .asciiz "  [Interrupt] "
__e1__:     .asciiz ""
__e2__:     .asciiz ""
__e3__:     .asciiz ""
__e4__:     .asciiz "  [Unaligned address in inst/data fetch] "
__e5__:     .asciiz "  [Unaligned address in store] "
__e6__:     .asciiz "  [Bad address in text read] "
__e7__:     .asciiz "  [Bad address in data/stack read] "
```

```
__e8_:      .asciiz "  [Error in syscall] "
__e9_:      .asciiz "  [Breakpoint] "
__e10_:     .asciiz "  [Reserved instruction] "
__e11_:     .asciiz ""
__e12_:     .asciiz "  [Arithmetic overflow] "
__e13_:     .asciiz "  [Inexact floating point result] "
__e14_:     .asciiz "  [Invalid floating point result] "
__e15_:     .asciiz "  [Divide by 0] "
__e16_:     .asciiz "  [Floating point overflow] "
__e17_:     .asciiz "  [Floating point underflow] "
__excp:     .word __e0_,__e1_,__e2_,__e3_,__e4_,__e5_,__e6_,
            __e7_,__e8_,__e9_
            .word __e10_,__e11_,__e12_,__e13_,__e14_,__e15_,
            __e16_,__e17_
s1:         .word 0
s2:         .word 0

.ktext 0x80000080
.set noat
# Because we are running in the kernel, we can use $k0/$k1 without
# saving their old values.
move        $k1, $at            # Save $at
.set at
sw          $v0, s1             # Not reentrant and we can't trust $sp
sw          $a0, s2
mfc0        $k0, $13            # Cause
```

```
mfc0        $k0, $13 Cause
sgt         $v0, $k0, 0x44      # Respond to interrupt exceptions
bgtz        $v0, _echo          # <<**** New Version ***********
```

```
addu        $0, $0, 0
li          $v0, 4              # syscall 4 (print_str)
la          $a0, __m1_
syscall
li          $v0, 1              # syscall 1 (print_int)
srl         $a0, $k0, 2         # shift Cause reg
syscall
li          $v0, 4              # syscall 4 (print_str)
lw          $a0, __excp($k0)
syscall
bne         $k0, 0x18, ok_pc    # Bad PC requires special checks
mfc0        $a0, $14            # EPC
and         $a0, $a0, 0x3       # Is EPC word aligned?
beq         $a0, 0, ok_pc
li          $v0, 10             # Exit on really bad PC (out of text)
syscall
```

```
######################## New Code ############################
_echo:
    li      $a0, 0xffff0000      # Base address of Memory-Mapped devices
    lw      $v0, 4($a0)          # Get Character from the Keyboard
    sw      $v0, 12($a0)         # Send Character to the Display
    b       ret
#############################################################
```

```
ok_pc:
    li      $v0, 4                   # syscall 4 (print_str)
    la      $a0, __m2_
    syscall
    mtc0    $0, $13                  # Clear Cause register
ret:
    lw      $v0, s1
    lw      $a0, s2
    mfc0    $k0, $14                 # EPC
    .set noat
    move    $at, $k1                 # Restore $at
    .set at
    rfe                              # Return from exception handler
    addiu   $k0, $k0, 4              # Return to next instruction
    jr      $k0
# Standard startup code.  Invoke the routine main with no arguments.
    .text
    .globl __start
__start:
    lw      $a0, 0($sp)              # argc
    addiu   $a1, $sp, 4              # argv
    addiu   $a2, $a1, 4              # envp
    sll     $v0, $a0, 2
    addu    $a2, $a2, $v0
    jal     main
    li      $v0 10
    syscall                          # syscall 10 (exit)
```

Floating-Point Instruction Set

Instruction	Syntax	
Absolute value double	abs.d	Fd, Fs
Absolute value single	abs.s	Fd, Fs
Add double	add.d	Fd, Fs, Ft
Add single	add.s	Fd, Fs, Ft
Branch if floating-point status flag is true	bc1t	label
Branch if floating-point status flag is false	bc1f	label
Compare and set flag if equal double	c.eq.d	Fs, Ft
Compare and set flag if equal single	c.eq.s	Fs, Ft
Compare and set flag if less than or equal double	c.le.d	Fs, Ft
Compare and set flag if less than or equal single	c.le.s	Fs, Ft
Compare and set flag if less than double	c.lt.d	Fs, Ft
Compare and set flag if less than single	c.lt.s	Fs, Ft
Convert single to double	cvt.d.s	Fd, Fs
Convert integer to double	cvt.d.w	Fd, Rs
Convert double to single	cvt.s.d	Fd, Fs
Convert integer to single	cvt.s.w	Fd, Rs
Convert double to integer	cvt.w.d	Rd, Fs
Convert single to integer	cvt.w.s	Rd, Fs
Divide double	div.d	Fd, Fs, Ft
Divide single	div.s	Fd, Fs, Ft
Load double (macro instruction)	l.d	Fd, address
Load single (macro instruction)	l.s	Fd, address
Load word into coprocessor 1	lwc1	Fd, offset(Rs)
Move double	mov.d	Fd, Fs
Move single	mov.s	Fd, Fs
Move from coprocessor 1	mdc1	Rd, Fs
Move double from coprocessor 1 (Macro Inst.)	mdc1.d	Rd, Fs
Move to coprocessor 1	mtc1	Fd, Rs
Multiply double	mul.d	Fd, Fs, Ft

Multiply single	mul.s	Fd, Fs, Ft
Negate double	neg.d	Fd, Fs
Negate single	neg.s	Fd, Fs
Store double (macro instruction)	s.d	Ft, address
Store single (macro instruction)	s.d	Ft, address
Store word from coprocessor 1	swc1	Fd, offset(Rs)
Subtract double	sub.d	Fd, Fs, Ft
Subtract single	sub.s	Fd, Fs, Ft

(Notice Fd, Fs, and Ft refer to the floating-point registers in coprocessor 1, which are designated in assembly language as $fn. Rs and Rd refer to registers in the general-purpose integer register file such as $a3.)

Index